# Answers
# To Your
# Questions
# About
# Homosexuality

# Answers To Your Questions About Homosexuality

Edited by
Cynthia Lanning

BRISTOL BOOKS
WILMORE, KY 40390

**BRISTOL BOOKS**
An imprint of Good News, A Forum for Scriptural Christianity, Inc.
308 East Main Street • Wilmore, KY  40390

# Contents

# 1

# The Facts About AIDS

## Susan S. Larson and David B. Larson

A group of infectious disease specialists from a number of hospitals met in 1980 to hear a baffling case presented by doctors at Georgetown University. A young man had died of a rare form of pneumonia. He had no known disease or exposures that could have led to this outcome. The assembled specialists were asked if any of them had ever encountered a similar case. Even though the physicians in that room represented hundreds of years of medical experience, all were baffled. None of those specialists could have suspected that this puzzling case was the harbinger of a deadly disease that would pervade the world during the next few years. The disease was AIDS—Acquired Immune Deficiency Syndrome. (The current scientific name for this disease is HIV infection—Human Immune Deficiency Virus. For the purpose of this chapter, the more commonly known acronym AIDS will be used.)

## Q
### Why do I need to learn about AIDS?

## A

To combat this disease it is first helpful to know specifics about the AIDS virus, how it debilitates the body and ways it spreads from one person to another.

Unknowns are scary. No wonder people become alarmed when a new, fatal disease is diagnosed. However, we all have a responsibility to understand the scope of the epidemic.

*Susan S. Larson is an independent writer and holds a Master of Arts degree in Teaching from Duke University. A former news staff writer, she received a first place award in news writing from the North Carolina Press Women's Association. David B. Larson, M.D., is a research psychiatrist and epidemiologist. An assistant professor at Duke University Medical Center, he also holds a Master of Science degree in Public Health from the University of North Carolina, Chapel Hill.*

Evidence shows the AIDS virus cannot be caught by casual contact. To assume that it is as infectious as the common cold is to place ourselves in the hands of fear and hysteria.

As Paul reminded Timothy, "Christ did not give us the spirit of fear, but of power, and love, and of sound mind." (2 Timothy 1:7 Phillips)

We need to use our sound minds to address the issues before us.

## Q

**How did this virus become so widespread so quickly in this country?**

## A

This disease was unwittingly transmitted from one person to another through sexual acts. As infected semen were passed from one body to another, the disease virus they contained went with them.

Those unknowingly infected in this way passed the virus to others by donating blood. Along with their gift of blood went the disease.

Others were unknowingly infected when they shared needles while injecting illicit drugs. Blood remaining on the needle from the infected person was shot into the needle user's veins along with the drug, and the disease went with it.

## Q

**How could people transmit this disease without knowing it?**

## A

AIDS often shows no signs of its presence until years after the person has been infected.

Though no symptoms may arise for months or years, once infected, the person can infect others. Since the person is unaware he or she is carrying the disease virus, the person is passing the disease virus along unwittingly.

For a number of years after it entered this country, AIDS was passed from one person to another through sex acts and contaminated blood before anyone knew the devastating disease even existed.

## Q

**How long does it take for AIDS symptoms to appear?**

## A

AIDS is a silent time bomb. It infects without any visible symptoms for at least six months, possibly for two to five years—and in some cases not for 15 or even 30 years.

Consequently, one can be infected for years without realizing it and pass it on to all sexual partners, who in turn pass it on to their sexual partners. Thus the disease spreads like a deadly pyramid scheme.

Even if a person does not develop the disease, once infected, that person becomes a carrier and can pass it on to others.

## Q
**Is there any hope that the spread of AIDS can be stopped?**

## A

Today the disease virus has been identified. Scientists have developed a blood test to screen for it and know it is spread through blood and sexual fluids. Because of this knowledge, the spread of AIDS can be stopped.

## Q
**Is AIDS a preventable disease?**

## A

Yes. Unless an individual has sex with an AIDS infected person or somehow has contact with infected blood, he or she is in no danger of getting the disease.

"For those who practice monogamy with the right person [one free from AIDS infection] this period of medical history will be relatively tranquil. For those who choose otherwise, it will be, increasingly, an age of anxiety," writes Dr. Bruce B. Dan.[1]

## Q
**Is AIDS still spreading?**

## A

Yes. It is still being transmitted as people engage in sex with persons who, unbeknownst to anyone, are infected with AIDS.

It is still spreading among drug abusers who share unsterilized needles. AIDS is also passed from infected mothers to their unborn children.

A killer without a cure thus far, the AIDS virus has mushroomed into a worldwide epidemic.

## Q
**How many people have the AIDS virus?**

## A

AIDS cases may reach one million wordwide by 1991, according to the World Health Organization estimates at the AIDS summit in London in January, 1988. AIDS cases have been reported in 114 countries and on all continents.

In the United States, the number of full-fledged AIDS cases has been doubling every 12 to 15 months since the disease was first identified in 1981.

## Q
**Does everyone who has the AIDS virus die of AIDS?**

## A
Not everyone infected with the AIDS virus develops the full-fledged disease, although possibly 30 percent or more will, according to the 1987 estimates.

Once infected, however, a person may progress to AIDS Related Complex, or "ARC," with symptoms of tiredness, weight loss, swollen lymph nodes and lowered resistance to infection.

Some of those persons with ARC—perhaps 30 percent of those initially infected—will eventually develop full-fledged AIDS. At that point their immune system is disabled. Unable to fight off usually dormant infections, their bo-

dies will eventually succumb to these now severe infections.

Meanwhile, these persons may or may not also suffer from AIDS-related dementia— a deterioration of the brain caused by the AIDS virus.

However at this point, anyone developing full-fledged AIDS usually dies within six to eighteen months.

## Q
**What is ARC (AIDS-Related Complex)?**

## A
ARC is a condition caused by the AIDS virus. Its symptoms are often less severe than those caused by classic AIDS or full-fledged AIDS. The person with ARC tests seropositive for AIDS infection and has symptoms similar to flu, except that they persist. These symptoms may include swollen lymph nodes (lymphadenopathy), weight loss, fever, night sweats, diarrhea, tiredness and lack of resistance to infection. Unfortunately, these are also signs of many other diseases.

## Q
**What is AIDS-related dementia?**

# A

In addition to destroying white blood cells which fight infection, the AIDS virus can also destroy brain tissue, leading to AIDS-related dementia. The virus travels along with the white blood cells into the cerebrospinal fluid and tissues of the brain. It infects nerve cells and causes them to become virus-producing factories. This destruction of brain tissue can cause depression, memory loss, loss of coordination, partial paralysis, decline of motor and sensory skills, change in concentration and personality.

The AIDS-related dementia is similar to what occurs when an elderly person becomes "senile" due to Alzheimers Disease. It involves progressive loss of memory, concentration and judgment. About two-thirds of AIDS patients suffer with AIDS-induced dementia. The severity of this problem varies. Some persons may find their judgment somewhat impaired while others become like late-stage Alzheimer patients, needing around the clock assistance.

This state of mind is not only difficult for the patient but also makes caring for them increasingly demanding.

# Q

**Who has AIDS?**

# A

In the United States, male homosexuals have contracted the disease most frequently. They account for 70 percent of all AIDS cases.

In Africa and Haiti, however, men and women have contracted the disease in equal numbers, indicating heterosexual transmission.

The greater the number of sexual partners one has, the greater the risk of exposure to the disease and hence the greater the risk of infection.

Very frequent sexual encounters among many homosexuals (having perhaps more than one hundred partners in a year or up to a dozen in a week according to some studies) has caused the disease to swiftly pervade this group. Current estimates are that 70 percent of the homosexual communities in New York and San Francisco are infected although many have not and may not develop the full-fledged disease. AIDS is the biggest killer of young men in those cities, outstripping any other cause of death.

In New York, AIDS also recently has become the biggest killer of young women, indicating the increase in heterosexual transmission.

## Q

**I'm not a homosexual, so should I really worry about AIDS?**

## A

AIDS is not only a blight on the homosexual community. Infected bisexual and heterosexuals alike can pass the AIDS virus to any sexual partners.

In the United States, four percent of AIDS cases were among heterosexuals in 1987. Although a small percentage, that group showed the largest increase, having escalated 131 percent since the previous year.

## Q

**Are many AIDS patients also drug abusers?**

## A

About 17 percent of AIDS cases in the U.S. have occurred among drug abusers. However, in most studies, if a person is a homosexual and a drug abuser he is counted in the homosexual column. In New York, which classifies AIDS

## What will the headlines say about AIDS in the 1990s?

❑ Since AIDS was first recognized in 1981, until June 1987, more than 36,000 persons in the U.S. have been diagnosed as having full-fledged AIDS. Half of those so diagnosed have died. As yet, the other half is also expected to die in the coming years.

❑ By 1991 a cumulative total of 270,000 cases will be diagnosed and 179,000 deaths will occur. This estimate is based on the fact that 1.5 million Americans are already infected with AIDS virus, according to the U.S. Public Health Service. In that year alone, an estimated 145,000 Americans will be ill with full-fledged AIDS and 54,000 will die—almost as many people as were killed in the Vietnam War.

❑ One health economist predicted that by 1991 AIDS patients will occupy more than one percent of the nation's total hospital beds—possibly five percent in New York and twelve percent in San Francisco.

❑ Total AIDS costs, including medical care and lost productivity due to disability and premature death, may surpass $66 billion per year in the next decade.

cases both ways, 30 percent of all AIDS cases can be traced to drug abuse.

# Q

**How does illegal drug use help spread AIDS?**

# A

AIDS spreads through the sharing of intravenous drug needles and syringes used for injecting illicit drugs. "Shooting up" drugs with unsterilized needles has brought the disease to an ever increasing number of drug abusers. Blood with virus from a person infected with AIDS that remains in the needle and is shot into another's vein effectively transfers the virus.

As a result, drug experts in New York City have estimated that 70 percent of addicts in that city are infected with the AIDS virus.

Drug users often engage in prostitution to get the money to support their expensive habit, creating an ever-widening cycle of becoming infected either through unsterilized needles or through multiple sexual contacts.

# Q

**Is it dangerous to receive donated blood?**

# A

Receiving blood from an infected donor can also transmit AIDS.

However, since March 1985 in the U.S. all donated blood has been tested for AIDS to virtually eliminate use of contaminated blood. Persons such as hemophiliacs who contracted AIDS from transfusions of contaminated blood products prior to that time account for about three percent of AIDS cases in the U.S.

All donated blood is tested for the presence of antibodies to the AIDS virus, which indicates exposure to the disease. However, because antibodies do not form immediately after exposure to the virus, a newly infected person may unknowingly donate blood after becoming infected but before his or her antibody test becomes positive. The U.S. surgeon general estimates this might occur now less than once in 100,000 transfusions.

# Q

**Why are all the future estimates about AIDS fuzzy?**

# A

Estimates about the future impact of AIDS are difficult because we still aren't sure what percentage of people who are infected with the disease will develop full-fledged AIDS. Current estimates are based on the historical fact that 20 to 30 percent of people who have the virus develop AIDS.

However, a recent study done in San Francisco showed that although the number of infected persons who develop full AIDS is fairly low during the first five years after infection, the number increases dramatically after the sixth year. Then well over half of those studied developed AIDS or AIDS-related diseases.

Since the disease has a long incubation period—a long time before symptoms occur after infection takes place—more time is needed to accurately chart the disease's progression.

Currently, the median time period from when infection occurs until the outbreak of symptoms is five to six years. However, symptoms may occur within two years, or possibly not for 15 to even 30 years.

## Q

**What are HIV, HTLV-III and LAV? Are they the same as AIDS?**

## A

The name AIDS stands for Acquired Immune Deficiency Syndrome. AIDS is the advanced stage of a disease caused by the AIDS virus. The virus has been given several different names, all of which indicate that it attacks certain white blood cells which help fight off infection. When these white blood cells are destroyed, the body is unable to fight off infections and becomes "Immune Deficient."

The scientific terms for the AIDS virus are HIV or HTLV-III or LAV. HIV means Human Immunodeficiency Virus and is its most recent name. HIV infection is the term currently used in the scientific literature.

Luc Montagnier and his colleagues at the Pasteur Institute in France in 1983 were the first to isolate the virus that causes AIDS. He named it LAV—Lymphadenopathy Associated Virus—because in many cases the virus causes swollen lymph glands.

The next year, 1984, Robert Gallo and his colleagues at the National Cancer Institute in Bethesda, Maryland, isolated the virus again and proved its association with AIDS. Gallo named the virus Human T-cell

Leukemia Virus(HTLV)-III because he thought it resembled the leukemia viruses, HTLV I and II. Since the virus does not cause leukemia, the L now stands for "lymphotropic" or "lymphocyte (white blood cell) seeking." The virus title became HTLV-III/LAV.

Gallo has subsequently discovered possible slight variants in the AIDS virus, expanding the HIV name to HIV-I and HIV-II. These variants have been contested by some scientists, who claim there is only one AIDS virus.

# Q
**How does the AIDS virus destroy the immune system?**

# A

When the AIDS virus invades the blood stream it attacks certain white blood cells called T-lymphocytes, or helper T-cells. The AIDS virus is a parasite that wants to convert these white blood cells into factories for producing more AIDS virus.

To retaliate against invasion the body produces antibodies to attack the AIDS virus. Usually an antibody will adhere strongly and kill a virus. But for some reason the antibodies that respond to AIDS adhere only half-heartedly,

and the virus wins, not only the battle but also the war.

AIDS virus is a "retrovirus." Its genetic material is RNA. When it invades the helper T-cells, it uses the cells to make DNA copies of its RNA. DNA serves as the human genetic recipe that tells the cell how to reproduce. In the conquered helper T-cells, however, the virus injects its own recipe as a substitute. Consequently, instead of creating more white blood cells needed to fight the infection, the helper T-cell makes AIDS virus particles according to the virus recipe.

The newly produced AIDS viruses from this white blood cell in turn invade more white blood cells to create more virus factories. As time goes on, more and more white blood cells are turning out viruses according to the virus recipe instead of the white blood cells the body desparately needs.

The role of the helper T-cell is to communicate between the cells that initiate the body's immune reaction and those that turn it off. Progressive loss of the helper T-cells due to AIDS virus attack increasingly disrupts the immune cycle. The body becomes less and less able to fight off infection.

If enough helper T-cells are destroyed, the body is "immune deficient" and falls prey to other diseases it could normally ward off. These diseases are called "opportunistic infections" since they seize the opportunity of lowered resistance to take hold. They have been more frequently seen in the end stages of cancers when the immune system is also depressed. It is these infections that the body is no longer able to fight off that do the killing.

# Q

**Why does AIDS often take so long to produce symptoms?**

# A

AIDS virus appears to be a "lentivirus"—a name derived from Latin *lentus*, meaning slow. The Lentiviruses, which infect sheep, goats and horses, are called this for their slow rate of reproduction. Lentiviruses produce from 40 to 400 new viruses in the same amount of time one normal flu virus needs to produce 2,000 new viruses.

Evidently, at some point in time, in some people, some unknown factor triggers the AIDS virus to crank up its production to extraordinary speeds. When that happens, an AIDS-invaded helper T-cell can then manufacture 40,000 new viruses in the same time the flu virus uses to make 2,000.

This extreme change in tempo explains why persons who are infected with the disease may have no symptoms for years, if ever. When their health appears normal the AIDS virus is reproducing very slowly. Some 80 to 90 percent of animals infected with lentiviruses stay well.

Of course, in some infected persons—currently the best estimate is about 30 percent— the AIDS virus does accelerate wildly, and the disease becomes full-blown. These persons die of infections that take hold once the immune system is wiped out.

# Q

**How can I find out whether or not I have the AIDS virus?**

# A

Screening and confirmatory blood tests can indicate whether a person has been infected with the AIDS virus long before any visible symptoms of the disease appear.

Once the AIDS virus enters a person's bloodstream, it attacks certain white blood cells, the helper T-cells, which are part of the body's defense system to fight off disease.

To retaliate, the body produces substances called antibodies to attack the invading AIDS virus (however, as explained earlier, these antibodies unfortunately are ineffective in destroying the AIDS virus).

If these AIDS virus antibodies are found in the blood, the person has tested "seropositive." He or she has been infected with the AIDS virus.

Unfortunately, it may take two weeks to three months for the body to produce enough antibodies to be detected with blood tests. Nevertheless, this is a much shorter time than the possible three to five years or longer that might pass before symptoms of the AIDS disease itself arise. At present only 30 percent of those who test seropositive are developing the full-fledged AIDS disease.

# Q

**Why is it important to test for AIDS?**

# A

The time may come when a blood test for AIDS may be required to obtain a marriage license, just as blood tests to detect other sexually transmitted diseases are mandatory. A marriage partner can not only pass the disease sexually to the spouse, but an infected parent has a 50 percent chance of passing the virus along to an unborn child.

During the 1987 International AIDS conference in Washington, D.C. a controversy arose about proposed mandatory AIDS testing of people in prison (where homosexual assaults can occur), hospital patients (so hospital staff can take particular precautions when dealing with AIDS-infected patients), as well as people seeking marriage licenses.

## How do people get AIDS?

The AIDS virus is not spread by casual contact, but by three specific means:

1) by intimate sexual contact which includes discharge of infected semen or vaginal fluid;

2) by blood stream contact with infected blood; and

3) from infected parent to unborn child.

AIDS is an infectious disease. It is contagious but does not spread like flu or measles. Casual contact living presents no risk of infection.

# Q

**What are symptoms of Classic or Full-fledged AIDS?**

# A

Full-fledged AIDS destroys a patient's immune system. Diseases the body otherwise could fight off invade the body. These are called "opportunistic infections" since they take advantage of the patient's weakened state to take hold.

One of the most common opportunistic infections is a fatal pneumonia (*Pneumocystis carinii*). Others include herpes, thrush, shingles, tuberculosis and toxoplasmosis.

Sometimes AIDS patients also develop a rare cancer of the blood vessels (*Kaposi's sarcoma*) which, along with other problems, causes purple blotches on the skin.

Patients may also have AIDS related dementia—cognitive, emotional and neurological problems resulting from the AIDS virus' destruction of brain tissue.

AIDS dementia can occur alone or with the immune deficiency.

Often a person with full-fledged AIDS shows rapid aging and "wasting" or weight loss.

Until a cure is found to revive the patient's immune system, patients with full-fledged AIDS will die of the opportunistic infections that take hold.

# Q

**What type of sexual contact spreads AIDS?**

# A

As U.S. Surgeon General C. Everett Koop points out, AIDS is contagious in the same way that sexually transmitted diseases like syphilis and gonorrhea are contagious: it is spread by intimate sexual contact (explicitly, penis-rectum, penis-vagina, mouth-rectum, mouth-vagina and mouth-penis).

During these sexual contacts, an infected person can exchange body fluids with another, thus transferring the virus.

# Q

**Do condoms prevent the spread of AIDS?**

# A

Use of condoms to prevent the exchange of body fluids during sex has been promoted to help curb infection. Although not a fail-safe method, condom use has been estimated to reduce risk tenfold.

# Q

## Why is AIDS more prevalent among homosexuals?

# A

Although AIDS virus can be transmitted heterosexually as well as homosexually, in the U.S. the current disease rate is highest among homosexuals.

Since first reported in 1981, AIDS has spread rapidly through the homosexual community for two reasons. First, many homosexuals tend to have a large number of partners, often several a week, thus increasing their risk of exposure to AIDS.

Second, the nature of homosexual acts among men allows the AIDS virus easier entry into the body. Infected semen deposited homosexually in another's rectum pass more easily through the rectum wall into the blood stream than they do through a woman's vaginal wall, which is thicker. Also, many homosexual acts are abrasive, creating tears and cuts which allow blood contact with the semen, providing the opportunity for the disease to pass more freely into the bloodstream. Furthermore, disease rates among homosexuals are high for other infections, such as Hepatitis B, which lowers resistance and makes infection from AIDS easier.

## It's easy to kill.

"This AIDS virus is highly specific to its niche, the helper T-cell," notes an epidemiologist at Johns Hopkins Hospital. "Outside that cell it doesn't survive well. It does not survive on toilet seats and doorknobs. A lot of things like drying, heat, sunlight, soap and water and alcohol kill it. It's easy to kill."

# Q

## What has AIDS meant to "sexual freedom"?

# A

The implications are clear: to avoid infection of AIDS one must refrain from promiscuous sexual behavior. Sexual contact with just one person can expose one to AIDS infection from any of that person's prior partners. Since AIDS symptoms may not appear for two to five years or longer, if ever, a person may easily infect another without realizing he or she is infected and a carrier.

Unfortunately, ceasing sexual activity for those emotionally addicted to promiscuous sexual behavior does not come easily, even though the known hazard of contracting AIDS is deadly.

# Q

## What happens when a woman with AIDS becomes pregnant?

# A

As AIDS has begun moving into the heterosexual community, infected mothers have begun passing the AIDS virus to their unborn children.

Studies show that from one-fifth to two-thirds of babies born to infected women will also be infected. These children usually die within a few years after their birth.

Care of these children entails huge costs. This is particularly evident in New York City where most U.S. AIDS babies are born.

U.S. Surgeon General C. Everett Koop advises women to see their doctor to be tested for AIDS if there is any chance they may have contracted the disease (1) through use of donated blood during a hospital stay prior to March 1985, (2) through shared drug needles or (3) by having sex with someone in an AIDS high risk group such as a bisexual male, a drug abuser, or a sexual partner of a drug abuser.

Today more than ever, men and women need to think twice before any premarital or extra-marital sexual encounter. They risk infecting their spouses and unborn children as well as themselves.

To date, in the U.S. almost all babies born with AIDS have been born to women who were intravenous drug users or sexual partners of intravenous drug users who were previously infected with the AIDS virus.

# Q

## Can casual social contact spread AIDS?

# A

No. AIDS virus is not transmitted through casual social contact. *Everyday living presents no risk to infection.*

U.S. Surgeon General C. Everett Koop explains this in his March 1986 Report:

Casual social contact such as shaking hands,

hugging, social kissing, crying, coughing or sneezing, will not transmit the AIDS virus. Nor has AIDS been contracted from swimming in pools or hot tubs or from eating in restaurants (even if a restaurant worker has AIDS or carries the AIDS virus). AIDS is not contracted from sharing bed linens, towels, cups, straws, dishes, or any other eating utensils. You cannot get AIDS from toilets, doorknobs, telephones, office machinery, or household furniture (p. 12).

Even family members living with persons who have AIDS do not become infected except through sexual contact.

# Q

## Do health care workers today risk contracting AIDS?

# A

Health care workers exposed to extremely sick AIDS patients have been studied and tested for infection with the AIDS virus. Some *25,000* doctors, nurses and other health care givers have been exposed to the AIDS patient's blood, stool and other body fluids such as tears and saliva. About 750 of these health care workers reported possible additional exposure through spills or being accidentally stuck with a needle. Upon testing, only *three* of those who stuck themselves with a needle had a positive antibody test for exposure to AIDS. None had developed the disease.

Since health care workers have much more intimate contact with patients and their body fluids than would be expected from normal, "everyday contact," and their risk of contracting AIDS is minute, we can feel confident the AIDS virus is not spread through casual contact.

# Q

## Is there a cure for AIDS?

# A

There is no known cure for AIDS, nor is there a vaccine to prevent it at this time.

Many experimental treatments are now being tested through the National Institutes of Health and pharmaceutical companies. One drug showing promising results is Azidothymidine (AZT). AZT inhibits the virus from duplicating itself. It does not kill the virus, however.

# Q

**How close are scientists to developing a vaccine to prevent AIDS infection?**

# A

The AIDS virus is difficult to vaccinate against since it undergoes extreme genetic variation. It changes as it reproduces in the body. A vaccine may be effective against one genetic strain but useless on a slightly different one.

Since the virus spends most of its time cloistered in the infected cells of its host, it is difficult to attack once infection is established.

# Q

**Is enough money available for AIDS research?**

# A

"We've got enough money to do the research that we are able to do right now," says U.S. Surgeon General C. Everett Koop. "We need not so much money as new ideas and new people."

He noted that from the day the hepatitis virus was identified until a vaccine was found took 19 years. "And that's an easy virus," he says.

"If every thing went smooth as glass, you might have a vaccine by 1995. People don't realize that if you get the wrong vaccine, that could produce all of the problems of the disease."

# Q

**How long has the AIDS virus been infecting humans?**

# A

The AIDS virus is a newcomer in human diseases. The first cases of AIDS virus infection in the U.S. appeared during the late 1970s, although the syndrome was yet undefined. At first, physicians thought they were dealing with a type of cancer.

Between 1976 and 1981 the disease in the U.S. was found almost exclusively among homosexual men. The connection between the practice of homosexuality and the disease was so strong it was initially called GRID for Gay Related Immunodeficiency Disease. The perception of AIDS as a homosexual disease has persisted in the U.S.

Later, the discovery of AIDS in hemophiliacs brought awareness that the virus could be transmitted through the blood supply.

By 1982 the AIDS virus was also showing its devastating

effects among intravenous drug users of both sexes, in infants of AIDS-infected parents and in a large group of Haitians, both men and women.

The acronym for the disease was thus changed from GRID to AIDS—Acquired Immune Deficiency Syndrome—pointing to infection beyond the homosexual community.

By 1983 the virus variously named LAV or HTLV-III was isolated and was proven in 1984 to be the cause of AIDS. The isolation and recognition was no small feat.

# Q

**How prevalent is AIDS outside the U.S.?**

# A

The first AIDS cases in Haiti, like those in the U.S., were primarily among homosexuals. However, bisexuality is more common in Haiti, and heterosexual contact between infected bisexual males and sexually active females spread the virus more widely in the population.

Among U.S. AIDS cases, men outnumber women 20 to 1. In Haiti the ratio will soon be 1 to 1.

The AIDS problem in Africa first became evident in 1982.

Physicians in Belgium began to see patients arriving for medical treatment from Zaire and Burundi with symptoms virtually identical to what was being called AIDS in the United States.

An investigation in the capital of Zaire by health agencies discovered that about 40 percent of the adults in the main hospital had diseases that were consistent with AIDS.

The pattern of the spread of AIDS in Africa to date has been much different than in the U.S. In Africa AIDS is found in men and women in equal numbers, similar to Haiti, again pointing to widespread heterosexual transmission.

In Western Europe, AIDS cases have now been reported in almost every country. The epidemic pattern there parallels but seems to lag behind that seen in the U.S. by several years.

# Q

**Where did the disease originate?**

# A

Immunologist Thomas Quinn suggests, "The best guess is the disease came from an animal— not necessarily from primates. This virus has relatives that cause diseases in lots of different animals."

The virus probably mutated and was then able to infect humans.

"Maybe someone got bitten, or got blood in a cut while butchering infected animals. The best guess is this happened in Central Africa," Quinn continues.

Speculating on the link between Africa, Haiti and the United States, Quinn notes, "In the early 1960s Zaire [formerly the Belgian Congo] became independent. It appealed to the U.N. [United Nations] for black, French speaking professionals to help with economic independence and Haiti responded.

"Haitians resided in Zaire, and some still do; but in the mid-70s, Zaire began nationalizing businesses and many Haitians left. Most went back to Haiti, but some went to the U.S. and some to Europe."

Also, in the 1970s Haiti was a popular vacation spot for homosexual men from the USA.

"We have no proof of any of this," observes Quinn. "This is our best guess because the virus has been found in those places, and because the times fit."

The fact that blood samples from the early 1970s in central Africa have shown a high incidence of AIDS antibodies underlies the assumption that the virus originated there. No serum samples stored in the United States prior to 1978 have been found to be seropositive.

At first the use and reuse of contaminated needles in certain tribal customs was cited as a possible factor in transmitting AIDS in Africa.

Some had also hypothesized that mosquitoes or other blood-sucking insects might be transmitting the disease.

However, researchers found that African AIDS patients were concentrated in the sexually active group of persons age 20 to 40. The mosquito hypothesis became untenable unless for some reason the insects only bit and infected people sexually active in that age range. These probabilities seem highly unlikely.

# Q

**How should Christians respond to the AIDS epidemic?**

# A

Statistics can tell us the number of people who potentially may die of AIDS.

Perhaps only the Holy

Spirit can measure the agony, hopelessness, fear, pain, anger, remorse and isolation those persons and their loved ones feel.

The Lord has placed each of us on this planet at this time in history for a reason.

He has entrusted us with the knowledge of His forgiveness and salvation and knowledge of the power of regeneration through his Holy Spirit.

As Christ's followers, we have the opportunity to help curb the growth of infection by not only emphasizing the physical dangers of promiscuity and drug abuse but also by offering an invitation to enter Christ's life-giving kingdom where such lifestyles are no longer appealing.

We have the chance to reach out to people overcome with illness, suffering and death and offer them physical help and comfort as well as the Word of Life.

As Christians, we can:

1) help to curtail the spread of AIDS;

2) help those in bondage to sexual behavior or drug abuse which places them at increased risk of infection; and

3) minister to those suffering with or dying from the disease.

## Q
**Why should we care about people who contracted AIDS because of their own bad choices?**

## A
Some may think those suffering from AIDS as a result of drug abuse, promiscuous sex or homosexual acts are finally paying for their immoral indulgences and are getting their just desserts.

But shouldn't we Christians realize that these people are ill with a fatal disease resulting from bondage to sex or drugs and serve them as Christ would serve the wounded, the broken and the dying?

We must face the fact that before accepting Christ our own sin—even though perhaps not placing us at risk of AIDS infection—nevertheless cut us off from God and was leading us to death.

"For all have sinned and fall short of the glory of God," Paul reminds us in Romans. "For the wages of sin is death, but the gift of God is eternal life in Christ Jesus our Lord."

## Q
**How can we know that God wants us to help people with**

**AIDS? After all, AIDS didn't exist in biblical times!**

# A

Jesus commanded us to be his witnesses to the ends of the earth and bring knowledge of His gifts of forgiveness, reconciliation and eternal life.

For some of us the most remote, undesirable place on earth may not be a faraway land with a strange name, but the call to minister to someone with the dreaded, sexually transmitted disease.

In Christ's day lepers were considered infectious untouchables. They were rejected, run from and relegated to the poorest of ghettos. Leprosy, like AIDS, was thought to spread through casual, social contact. Leprosy, like AIDS, did not spread through casual social contact.

But Christ ignored this social code. He talked to, touched and healed lepers—individually and in groups.

At the start of His ministry He used the words of Isaiah to announce his mission,

"The Spirit of the Lord is upon me, because he has anointed me to preach good news to the poor. He has sent me to proclaim release to the captives and recovering of sight to the blind, to set at liberty those who are oppressed" (Luke 4:18).

We know that AIDS does not spread through casual social contact, so those who minister to AIDS victims are not placing themselves or their families at risk. We can run from persons with AIDS as though we are the Pharisees and they are as the lepers of the past, or we can minister to their needs.

As more and more people suffer with this disease, now is the time to decide what we can do and what we want to do.

As Christ's servants we have the chance to share the light of His kingdom by our example of love and care.

# Q

**How can Christians help?**

# A

**➻ 1) By educating youth.**

Young people need to know explicitly how to avoid infection with the AIDS virus.

This calls for an understanding of the disease and its methods of transmission: intimate sexual contact and blood to blood contact.

Younger people often feel invulnerable to disaster. They assume it might happen to someone else but never to them. Their sense of false invulnerability can be seen in the high rates of pregnancy and auto accidents among teenagers.

They may feel more tempted to experiment with drugs, premarital sex or homosexuality than other age groups.

Scripture clearly forbids sexual immorality and abusing one's body. Making sure teens clearly know what the word of God says on these subjects is crucial.

The scriptural wisdom of sex only within marriage is underscored in an editorial of the *Journal of the American Medical Association.*

"Absolutely safe sex is that within a mutually monogamous relationship in which neither person carries the virus," writes Dr. Bruce B. Dan.[2]

The disease AIDS may be a rather abstract concept to young people. Reviewing a book such as *A Colour Atlas of AIDS: Acquired Immunodeficiency Syndrome* can give them an eye-opening view of the horrible effects of the diseases which ravage the body after AIDS destroys the immune system. Like the vivid car crash films shown in driver's education classes to promote safety, books like this can make real the potential disaster of risking AIDS infection.

They must also learn that having sex and "shooting up" drugs puts them at high risk of infection.

Even ear piercing can result in infection if the needles are unclean. Seek out a doctor or nurse to pierce ears to make sure sterilized needles are used.

Most of all, young people must be shown that a relationship with Jesus Christ gives lasting meaning, direction and fulfillment to life and is the most powerful antidote to desires for drugs or sex.

**➠2) By caring for caregivers.**

In some churches, groups are organizing to help families and homes caring for AIDS patients. Some of these groups deliver in meals. Others provide babysitting or housekeeping. Still others gather supplies and deliver them. The church can demonstrate Christ's love by sharing the burden of care.

**➠3) By supporting Christian ministries to homosexuals, drug abusers and prostitutes.**

A number of Christian ministries reach out to homosexuals, drug abusers and prostitutes whose sexual and drug practices put them at high risk for AIDS infection. Once engaged in, these life-styles are difficult to escape. Some wanting to change feel impotent to achieve success. The good news of Christ's love, forgiveness and regeneration, plus the loving support these ministries give, can help people in these high-risk groups find an alternative life-style that is not only healthier but also filled with more joy and peace.

**⁕ 4) By helping infants and toddlers abandoned by AIDS-infected mothers in city hospitals.**

Some of these AIDS infected children never travel beyond the walls of a hospital before they die. Churches can help improve their quality of life, if only by donating toys and clothing.

In some cases Christian families have adopted these children in true sacrificial love.

**⁕5) By bolstering the health care system.**

The escalating number of AIDS patients and the high cost of their care will continue to exact an ever increasing toll on the health care system.

The average stay for an AIDS patient is 30 days, compared with eight for other patients.

As more hospital beds are filled with AIDS patients, less room is left for treating other health problems.

The average cost of care ranges from $35,000 to $50,000 per AIDS patient. Though some patients have health insurance, many, especially drug abusers, do not. Costs will be borne by government, hospitals and communities.

At least $40.5 billion will be spent between 1987 to 1991 on AIDS patient treatment, estimates the Health Insurance Association of America. By other national estimates it could reach two or three times more.

Now is the time to prepare for this healthcare space and cost crisis.

Churches can plan and set up homes and hospices to provide care for the dying.

Dr. Charles Levy, chief of the infectious disease section at Washington Hospital Center, noted the need for preparation in Washington, D.C. and other cities around the country: "Even if the numbers remain as low as we could possibly hope for, the impact on these cities and these hospitals and this community will be staggering. We can't do enough to be prepared for what's coming."

# A nurse tells what it is like to care for AIDS patients

After caring for AIDS patients during the past five years, an experienced Christian nurse research specialist at the National Institutes of Health, shares some of her insights:

When a person faces death, questions about the meaning of life rise to the forefront. The less important issues fade away. No time or energy remains for pre-occupation with lesser things.

Patients who have been told they will soon die ask four questions:

*Who am I?*

*Why was I created and by whom?*

*Have I accomplished my purpose?*

*If not, is there time left to do so?*

"It's a one-on-one struggle with God, even as those around clean the bed and help get groceries," she explains.

"Unless the people reaching out have explored and answered those questions for themselves, they cannot help the dying AIDS patient in their spiritual distress," she notes. "Unless the caregivers have their own spiritual roots, they will avert their eyes and become uncomfortable and embarrassed when the patient asks such questions."

The caregiver needs to ask himself or herself, where am I coming from? Why do I want to help? What do I hope to give them?

"If you think you are going there to throw the first stone, then you don't know who you are in Christ," she adds. If you want to go to bring the character of God, then you have to have God's character, which is love not condemnation.

"Many patients already feel like they have been judged." Many don't want to see clergy. Some feel they have failed God, that their sin is too great for Him to forgive. Others are angry, believing they were born homosexual and cannot change.

All have horror stories of friends or former lovers dying.

Cancer patients have long taught us "Don't take away my hope. . .Don't leave me alone to die," she says. The dying person hopes for comfort, hopes for care, hopes for cure.

Because of the stigma of their disease, AIDS patients often don't have the support groups other dying patients might have. Their lovers may have died. Or perhaps they don't want to tell their lover and be abandoned or tell anyone and risk losing their job and their source of income.

As the disease progresses those with AIDS become increasingly unsightly. Those with *Kaposi's sarcoma* at first try to hide the lesions with make-up. Then they grow facial hair. Eventually they can't cover their lesions and feel more and more socially isolated. At some point they may have lesions everywhere and are struggling for breath.

One way to help these patients is to locate significant others from their past and urge attempts at reconciliation while the patient still has energy. At first they may not want to rebuild those burned bridges, but as strength fails and they realize they are dying, they often want to renew those ties. The nurse explains that many AIDS patients she has known had stopped talking to their parents 10 to 15 years before.

"Help them accomplish some things they feel are important," she says. "Allow them as much control as you can so they retain a sense of personal dignity."

AIDS and the suffering and death it brings launch patients into spiritual crisis.

"I've blown it. You're only given one chance and I've blown it," one patient cried out to the nurse as he wept.

After many hours of the nurse and a pastor discussing the love of Jesus, the patient accepted Christ's love and forgiveness. He entrusted his life to Jesus Christ.

"This man radiated Christ's love, despite his unsightly lesions," she recalls. "His mother, in her 80s, came to see him. She came to the Lord the morning before he died. That gift was given to him.

"As we share in the intimacy of the dying experience and their sufferings, we strongly feel that otherwise elusive concept of living in the moment, moment by moment," the nurse observes. "Too often we forget that we are all dying. That is the gift they give to us."

---

# Q

**What can I do if I am not emotionally, spiritually or physically equipped to reach out to AIDS patients?**

# A

We can commit ourselves to pray for these patients.

We can help fund supplies for hospices, help organize volunteers or lend support in other ways. AIDS has opened a cavern of devastation that only Christ's love can fill.

The decision to serve as a nurse to AIDS patients didn't come easily to this nurse, even though she had been caring for terminally ill cancer patients for years.

*Kaposi's sarcoma*, a cancer of the blood vessels, is one disease AIDS patients may get once their immune system weakens. The nurse was facing treating these cancer patients who also have AIDS.

She was angry. She did not want to be exposed to these patients. They were the untouchables.

"Lord, I've always cared for terminally ill patients. Why am I now saying no?" she asked herself.

She fought and wrestled with this issue in prayer. After a while a wave of realization hit her.

"*These* are not the least of mine" she could hear the Lord telling her. These patients with AIDS were not the least— not the lowest of the low.

"We are all the lowest of the low before the Lord. We all sin and fall short of God's intentions [Rom. 3:23]. We are not to judge," she realized. "Each of us is the 'least'. We are each to

repent and receive forgiveness."

She then felt free to serve these AIDS patients.

Her blood tests show no sign of infection with the disease.

> *"Lord, when did we see you hungry and feed you, or thirsty and give you something to drink? When did we see you a stranger and invite you in, or needing clothes and clothe you? When did we see you sick or in prison and go to visit you?"*
>
> *The King will reply, "I tell you the truth, whatever you did for one of the least of these brothers of mine, you did for me."*

**Free AIDS Information by Phone:**

**AIDS Hotline of the Public Health Service: 1-800-342-AIDS**

**Drug Abuse Treatment Information: 1-800-662-HELP**

**AZT information: 1-800-843-9388**

# 2

# What the Old Testament Says About Homosexuality

## Edited by Cynthia Lanning

The Old Testament view of homosexuality cannot be understood without knowing something about the Bible's view of sexuality itself. The first questions and answers deal with such background information.

**Q**

**What is the Old Testament view of God and sexuality?**

**A**

To appreciate the uniqueness of the biblical truth that God is not a sexual being, one must read the pagan mythologies from around the world. First of all, the myths say the gods got here just as the rest of us did—through sexual procreation. They were sexually generated out of chaos, and those first gods then generated others. But the Bible makes it plain that God was neither sexually generated, nor did He so generate anything else. He is not continuous with the created system. The language of sexuality simply is not applicable to Him.

*Cynthia Lanning* is a Christian writer living in Cincinnati, Ohio. This chapter is based on research by *Dr. John Oswalt*, Professor of Old Testament and Semitic Languages at Trinity Evangelical Divinity School, Deerfield, Illinois. He received his A.B. degree from Taylor University, Upland, Indiana; his B.D. and Th.M. degrees from Asbury Theological Seminary; and his M.A. and Ph.D. degrees from Brandeis University.

This recognition is very important for the current sexist debate. While God's roles are commonly defined in male terms, His nature never is. His genitalia are never described; His couplings with consorts—divine, human or animal—are never mentioned; He is never defined as sexually male. He is not a sexual being.

## Q

**But if this is so, why are God's roles more often described in male terms? If it is true that God has no sex, shouldn't we begin to describe Him also in female terms for the sake of balance?**

## A

I think not. There are two reasons for this. One is practical, the other more theoretical.

The practical reason is that around the world mother cults are almost exclusively fertility-oriented. Motherhood and childbearing are all but synonymous. Thus to call God "Our Mother in heaven," given our human tendency to make sex sacred anyway, opens real doors to the sexualizing of God. Obviously many male deities also are associated with fertility cults but by no means all.

Apparently maleness is not so completely tied to reproduction in the human mind as is femaleness. For this reason then male terms are more practical to describe the transcendent God. They are less prone to become entangled with sexuality.

The theoretical concern relates to our freedom to rewrite biblical figures of speech. Obviously everything said in human speech about the infinite God must use images. The most we can say is, "God is like—," or "God acts like—," all the time knowing that the One-Who-Is is as far beyond our little images as the sun is beyond a speck of dust. But does this recognition leave us free to replace the biblical figures with new ones as situations change? I think not. Figures of speech are not totally divorced from the realities they represent.

## Q

**The Bible seems vague about many specific issues, so shouldn't we use situation ethics as a more realistic guide to practical daily living?**

## A

Those who are confident that

the Bible is the Word of God can approach it regarding any issue of life. In some cases, no specific word is given. This does not, however, permit us to disregard the Bible and do what we wish. Rather it calls us to the difficult task of sorting out other evidence, drawing implications and coming to a conclusion that will provide the basis for our practice as faithful followers of the living God.

Such conclusions must always admit the possibility of contrary judgments. The matter of smoking is an example. The Bible speaks no specific word on this issue. But by the process just outlined many have come to the conviction that smoking cigarettes is always wrong in God's sight. This may be so, but lacking a specific word from the Bible itself, we must allow the possibility of smoking cigarettes being acceptable in some circumstances.

The matter of homosexuality is different. It is evident from numerous clear statements in the Bible, and even more numerous allusions, that homosexual acts are never right. On this issue there is simply no other answer for those who submit their ethical decisions to the authority of Scripture.

Situation ethics has been destructive regarding such clear ethical teaching. Through the use of bizarre scenarios, such as the famous prison camp episode (in which a woman wonders whether she could justify having relations with a man on the grounds that she would be released if she became pregnant), it is suggested that the ethical norms that govern our daily lives are always up for renegotiation. Whatever the good intentions of the situationists may have been, the actual result of their teaching has been the erosion of ethical standards in daily living as more and more persons find "good" reasons—usually hedonistic and self-serving—for disobeying clear scriptural teaching.

# Q

**Why should we be concerned about what the Old Testament might say about homosexuality? Don't we follow the New Testament's "more excellent way of love"?**

# A

Some people may say, "The idea of absolute ethical standards is an Old Testament point of view. I submit to the authority of Scripture, but it is the authority of the New Testament. The only prescription in the New Testament is love. Whatever is the loving thing to do, that is right."

This distorts New Testament teaching. To be sure, the New Testament teaches that love is the highest motive for action. But the popular situationists' rationale sets up a false dichotomy. The choice is not between loveless standards and a loving lack of standards. The choice the New Testament offers so forcefully is: obedience to God's standards for the right reason (love) or obedience for the wrong reason (self-righteousness). The New Testament does not cancel the standards of the Old Testament by its teachings on love. Rather, it denounces a person's patting himself on the back for a rigid observance of certain commands when his heart is empty and cold.

## Q

**What is the Old Testament view of human sexuality?**

## A

In the first chapter of Genesis the basic fact of human life is asserted—that we are sexual beings, male and female. Why are we this way? The question is answered in the next breath—in order to reproduce ourselves. The fundamental purpose of our sexuality, though by no means the only purpose, is reproduction. This first biblical statement about sex, occurring as it does in the first biblical statement about humanity, makes it abundantly clear that whatever understanding of sexuality we have, we cannot denounce the male/female function of childrearing and parenting.

## Q

**Does the Old Testament explain why God created humans as male and female? Why didn't He create us all male or all female?**

## A

Not only did God make us to reproduce, which assumes male and female, He also made us male and female for each other. The second chapter of Genesis spells this out in a way that is simple enough for a five-year-old to grasp but profound enough to engage the most mature scholar.

It is not good for a person to be alone, says the writer. All of us can attest to that out of our own experiences. The question is, however, what is God's intended solution for that loneliness? What does Adam need? Does he need companionship, friendship? Yes, but his needs are deeper than that. He needs someone to whom he can belong and to whom he can give himself physically.

Most significantly, Adam is involved in the search. So always God preserves our dignity and insures the depth of our understanding by letting us discover what He already fully knows. The animals are led before Adam. God gives him the opportunity to define the problem and discover the solution, if he can. What he discovers is that the male, by himself, is not complete. If he were, he could bask in that perfect communion with God that was his birthright and need no one else. But after all the animals have paraded past him, Adam knows what God knew—someone is missing.

The words *it is not good* in this context are important (Gen. 2:18). All through the first chapter of Genesis the recurring refrain has been, "And God saw that it was good" (vss. 10, 12, 18, 25). These are the words of an artist. In his mind he has envisioned something.

Now he has transferred that onto paper or canvas or stone. If the outcome corresponds to the vision, his response is "That's good." But if it does not correspond, what then? Exactly what God said about Adam's aloneness.

Adam's aloneness was not the way God had envisioned humanity. The male was not enough to complete the full concept of "man." He could not, by himself, be a full person. Someone else was needed so that he, together with that other person, could know what it means to be fully human. That full humanity could not be attained through the creation of another male. The Creator's vision of full humanity was of two sexually differentiated components, each of the same stuff, on a par, the same, yet different, finding their fulfillment in mutual surrender. Adam's ecstatic response to Eve's creation was, in effect, "This is me, yet, glory to God, it's not me."[1]

# Q

**Does the Old Testament teach us that sex is just for reproduction—or are humans supposed to enjoy sex?**

# A

The Old Testament understanding of our sexuality—that it is not fundamental to the universe but that it is fundamental to human make-up—means several things. Above everything else, it means that, within the bounds of mutual male/female commitment, we are called to a frank enjoyment of our sexuality.

Sex is not the key to existence. It is not the source of our ultimate meaning. Sex is simply one more part of God's good creation—a significant part, to be sure, and a highly charged part— but not the be-all and end-all of human existence.

The Bible clearly declares that sex is a delightful gift intended to be enjoyed. Proverbs 5-7 contains the best statement of this from the male point of view. The passage encourages a man to delight in his wife's charms, to drink deeply from her as from a well. It also warns him that if he thinks the adventuress can give more lasting satisfaction, he is mistaken.

By the same token the Song of Solomon (known to the Jews as the Song of Songs, or "best song of all") which depicts a male's uninhibited delight in his partner, also depicts the female's delight in him. That delight is a long way from the caricatured Victorian lady passively allowing her husband to use her while she thinks of other, more pleasant things. Our sexuality is God's good gift to us.

# Q

**If God who created us wants us to take pleasure in our sexuality, why does He give us rules like those in the Old Testament that restrain our enjoyment of sexuality?**

# A

To use our sexuality in ways that do not accord with the Creator's character and the nature and purpose of the world is to court disaster.

Notice that God sets the boundaries outside of heterosexual marriage. Within such marriage there is virtually complete freedom.

Some states' statute books still contain laws that regulate how often and in what positions a married couple may enjoy sex. The Bible will have no part of this. To be sure, the Bible rules out of bounds those uses of sex that will enslave and destroy. But within the boundaries there is freedom to trust, explore and give. The Lawgiver is not some prurient person who, in the words of the late Paul Little, scurries around looking for someone who is having fun so He can shout, "Now you cut that out!" He does not seek to regu-

---

## What exactly does the Old Testament say about homosexual behavior?

The Torah (the laws contained in the Old Testament) contains two explicit prohibitions of homosexual behavior. These are found in the book of Leviticus at 18:22 and 20:13. With their immediate contexts, they read:

"Do not approach a woman to have sexual relations during the uncleanness of her monthly period. Do not have intercourse with your neighbor's wife and defile yourself with her. Do not give any of your children to be sacrificed to Molech, for you must not profane the name of your God. I am the Lord. Do not lie with a man as one lies with a woman; that is detestable. Do not have sexual relations with an animal and defile yourself with it. A woman must not present herself to an animal to have sexual relations with it; that is a perversion. Do not defile yourselves in any of these ways, because this is how the nations that I am going to drive out before you became defiled. Even the land was defiled; so I punished it for its sin, and the land vomited out its inhabitants" (18:19-25).

"If a man sleeps with his daughter-in-law, both of them must be put to death. What they have done is a perversion; their blood will be on their own heads. If a man lies with a man as one lies with a woman, both of them have done what is detestable. They must be put to death; their blood will be on their own heads. If a man marries both a woman and her mother, it is wicked. Both he and they must be burned in the fire, so that no wickedness will be among you. If a man has sexual relations with an animal, he must be put to death, and you must kill the animal. If a woman approaches an animal to have sexual relations with it, kill both the woman and the animal. They must be put to death; their blood will be on their own heads. . . Keep all my decrees and laws and follow them, so that the land where I am bringing you to live may not vomit you out. You must not live according to the customs of the nations I am going to drive out before you. Because they did all these things, I abhorred them" (20:12-16, 22-23).

late and inhibit every action. Rather He is the benevolent Father who delights in His children's enjoyment and only wants them to know where the dead-end roads lie.

# Q

**Why were the entire passages from Leviticus quoted above instead of just the parts pertaining to homosexual behavior?**

# A

The context of these passages is very significant. Both of them deal with the sexual practices of Israel's neighbors-to-be. Homosexuality is not singled out. It is but one part of a whole package. The prohibition of homosexual behavior is not simple "homophobia," that is, an irrational fear of a practice we do not understand. Rather, it is part of a *total* approach to sexuality, an approach that denies any boundaries in creation and uses sex as a vehicle to make that statement. Homosexuals are not being singled out as an oppressed minority.

# Q

**Why do humans' sexual practices matter to God at all?**

# A

There is a certain mystic sense to human sexuality, as the Bible sees it. The copulation of a woman and a man is of a different order than that of a cow and a bull. Genesis 2:24 gives us the first inkling of this when it says, "For this reason (the fact that a man and a woman are made for each other) a man will leave his father and mother and be united to his wife, and they will become one flesh."

The sex act culminates that process whereby two sexually different partners are melded together into one new personality. Now sex, in and of itself, cannot produce that melding of personalities the Bible talks about. Sex has no power in itself. A wife separated from her husband told me recently that whenever they got back together they had great sex experiences, but that didn't solve their problem. And so it cannot. Sex must be the symbol of something that has taken place and is taking place. This is a part of God's lovely plan for us, not only in the expression of our sexuality but also in general. He has made us so that what we do with our bodies demonstrates the expression of our spirits.

# Q

**Why does the Old Testament demand commitment in sexual relationships?**

# A

The mystical power of sexuality to somehow bring to fulfillment the reality of commitment and self-giving explains why the language of love and marriage provides some of the deepest metaphors for the relation of God to human beings. Where can we find better imagery to express God's concern for us? He delights in us as a lover in the beloved. He finds us as ravishing as does a groom his bride. He longs for us to know Him, as He knows us. He has committed Himself to us as irrevocably as Hosea did to his wife even though she forsook him for prostitution.

Let it be said again—this is all metaphor, a figure of speech, conveying a deeper truth. God is not actually male, nor is Israel or the church actually female. But the experiences of love and marriage provide the best vehicle for beginning to understand what His love is like.

This rooting of the sex experience in commitment and self-disclosure explains why adultery is the worst of all sexual sins in the biblical catalog. It is a denial of commitment, a breaking of faith and an act of treachery (cf. Mal. 2:13-15). This is why the commandment singles out adultery for attention.

So the Bible portrays sex as given for the purposes of reproduction and for the achievement of human completion. It serves as a vehicle to teach the truths of submission, faithfulness, commitment and experiential knowledge.

# Q

**Aren't the Israelites' rather strict sexual mores simply those of a rural, provincial people? Urban people around the world have broader sexual tolerance. So, don't biblical sexual standards really only represent a subculture?**

# A

How long was Israel rural anyway? The great prophets of the northern kingdom spoke to a culture that had been urban and cosmopolitan for five hundred years. They themselves grew up in that culture. Yet they did not tolerate the steady influx of Canaanite morals and manners. Their world view, not their culture, shaped their preaching.

The pagans themselves recognized that their practices were dangerous to society at large. Heterosexual marriage was a practical necessity for societal stability. Thus homosexuality, though practiced somewhat widely in Egypt and Mesopotamia and more widely in Greece and Rome, was technically illegal in all those countries.

# Q

**What if a person honestly cannot help having homosexual urges? Does the Old Testament condemn people for homosexual feelings?**

# A

No. These Scriptures forbid homosexual *behavior*. Neither here nor anywhere else in Scripture are persons said to be "bad" because they feel an attraction to a person of the same sex. This is a very significant aspect of the biblical understanding of human nature. While we are not responsible for our predilections, our behavior can transcend our feelings. This point of view is in strong opposition to prevailing behavioral theory today, a theory that argues that we have no real control over our behavior.

# Q

**Aren't we programmed by our heredity and environment to behave in certain ways, like it or not? Couldn't a homosexual person rationalize: "I didn't ask to be this way; so it's not my fault. The people who influenced me probably didn't know what they were doing either; so, it's not their fault. It is nobody's fault, and if it's nobody's fault, it can't be wrong"?**

# A

The Bible directly opposes this point of view. It offers the possibility of transcending heredity and environment. Of course heredity and environment influence us, but they do not determine us. We have a real choice whether to actualize the image of the transcendent Creator in us or to further deface that image. Surely this invests the word "human" with a grandeur and a dignity that is sadly lacking in the philosophies of today.

The Bible offers us the freedom *not* to act out our feelings. Consider the story of Cain and

Abel. Cain did not have to act out the anger he felt. It did not have to master him as, for instance, Esau's anger did not master him. Thus when Cain failed to control his anger, he was responsible for his action. But the initial feeling of anger was not the sin. The sin was in surrendering to that feeling.

# Q

**Do Old Testament prohibitions against homosexuality have universal force? Is it possible that they were valid for that time and place but of no significance for today? For instance, the law specifically forbids the eating of pig meat, yet most Christians eat pork today with no flicker of conscience. Why should we regard the prohibition of homosexual behavior any differently?**

# A

First of all it is important to understand what the law is. The historical context is crucial to such an understanding.

By the time of the Red Sea crossing, both the Egyptians and the Hebrews knew that they had not encountered some localized Midianite mountain god. This being was God. But beyond His overwhelming power, who was He? God's purpose of self-disclosure had only begun. How could he show the Hebrews, and through them the world, that He is not simply power but, more importantly, integrity, faithfulness, consistency and love, and that true godlikeness, or holiness, consists of these? He did so by entering into a binding agreement, or covenant, with the Hebrew people. The law functions as a part of the total covenant document.

The covenant went something like this. "I agree to be your God. I commit Myself to you to care for you, defend you and bless you. You agree to be My people. You must therefore live lives like Mine. You must. . . ." Then follow the Ten Commandments, which are a short form of the stipulations of the covenant. The rest of the law is a fleshing out of the meaning and implications of the commandments. Its purpose is to teach what God and His world are like.

The fleshing out of the law is recorded in the remainder of Exodus, Leviticus, parts of Numbers and all of Deuteronomy. It includes three kinds of materials: instructions concerning civil life, instructions concerning religious ceremony and worship and instructions concerning moral life. The latter give us direct moral teaching as found, for example, in the Ten Commandments. Those in the former categories teach moral principles through certain kinds of behavior. These kinds of behavior may no longer be relevant, but the principles still are.

# Q

**I still don't understand why the civil and ceremonial Old Testament laws apply only to that day and age while the moral laws are for all time.**

# A

The law teaches certain principles about the nature of God and His world. The ceremonial and civil parts teach those principles through requirements that are temporary. The civil law speaks to specific behaviors in that society, many of which are no longer practiced, and the ceremonial law calls for symbolic behaviors whose symbolism is no longer necessary. For example, the defiling and contaminating power of sin is real; however, dietary laws are no longer needed, or should no longer be needed, to teach that point. By the same token, there is still no forgiveness of sin without the shedding of blood, but in the light of the cross we should hardly need the death of animals to understand that truth.

However in the third part of the law, the behaviors called for or prohibited are neither symbolic nor limited to a certain time and place. These teachings have been called the moral law. In these the behavior and the principle are synonymous, and they are for all people in all time. There are no qualifiers and no conditions. These laws are simply what those who are rightly related to God will do.

# Q

**Aren't we just picking and choosing when we say the Old Testament has different kinds of law? How can we be sure we know which laws are civil or ceremonial (and thus may not apply today) and which are moral (and do apply today)?**

# A

The distinction is not nearly so difficult to draw as some suggest today. In fact in most cases it is quite clear.

The civil law in particular is relatively easy to spot. It commonly deals with specific cases of civil life such as the borrowing of another's tools (Exod. 22:10-13) or regulations concerning slavery (Deut. 15:12-18).

Likewise the ceremonial law is relatively easy to recognize: it usually regards the form and use of ceremonies or ceremonial structures. Such laws define actions or events that render one unclean for ceremonial purposes, such as the handling of the dead, having any hemorrhage or emission from the body, eating unclean food and so forth. Each of these prevents one from taking part in the ceremonies for a stated time but has no other penalty.

Certain other actions, however, do not pertain to the just functioning of society or the maintenance of the ceremonies. They are commonly stated in categorical imperatives, and the punishment, when prescribed, is death. These wrongdoings are viewed as offenses against God or against life itself. Such, for example, is the cursing of one's mother or father (Lev. 20:9) or the offering of sacrifice to an idol (17:1-9). These offenses are not related to either civil or ceremonial behavior. They do not render one unclean or re-

quire the payment of a fine. Rather these misdeeds are wrong at any time in any place. To suggest that these actions, which carry the death penalty, are of no greater significance than the eating of pork, which only renders one ceremonially unclean, betrays a serious misunderstanding of the biblical statements.

# Q

**Couldn't the injunction against homosexual behavior have been included simply to teach the Hebrew people to be different from their heathen neighbors?**

# A

The prohibitions of homosexual behavior are stated as moral law. Such behavior is categorically prohibited and the death penalty is prescribed. There are no relative conditions. To be sure, the commands are part of a comprehensive sexual ethic that contradicts the pagan practices. However the rationale behind that ethic is not simply reaction to a lifestyle that happens not to be Hebrew. In other words, these commands are not given just so Israel's national identity will be distinct from that of its neighbors.

# Why doesn't the Old Testament specifically prohibit lesbianism?

Only male homosexuality is specifically prohibited in the Old Testament. Lesbianism is not mentioned. From this observation some have concluded that the commandment against homosexuality is primarily concerned with the degradation of a male. It is suggested that the Bible opposes male homosexuality because it drags a male down to the level of a female. The commandment, then, is the work of a male-sexist society that does not care whether sexual relations between members of the same sex occur but cares very deeply whether a male is treated like a female. Therefore, some argue, since we are now Christians and do not regard treating a male like a female as being degrading, homosexual behavior among males is permissible, as it always has been among females.

This novel interpretation is an argument from silence: since the Bible is silent about lesbianism, lesbianism is permissible. But there are a number of other, more likely, explanations for this omission. For instance, opportunities for lesbian encounters were limited in the ancient New Eastern societies where a woman's movement outside the home was somewhat restricted. Also there may have been little need for a command relating especially to women because women in the ancient world expected to find their life's fulfillment in the bearing and raising of children. The absence of lesbian behavior in the temples probably supports this hypothesis.

The ancient pagan world exalted the female principle to the heights but trampled actual women in the mud. By contrast the Old Testament treats women with remarkable respect. To be sure, the Old Testament position is not as fully developed as that of the New. For instance, in the Old Testament a woman could be treated as having less economic worth than a man. But over all she is given equal personal worth. In fact many of the laws that feminists regard as sexist are precisely the laws that guaranteed the rights and the dignity of a woman in those cultural circumstances (for instance, her right to refrain from intercourse during menstruation and her right to demand that her brother-in-law fulfill his conjugal obligations in place of her dead husband).

In conclusion, there is no reason to imagine that homosexuality is forbidden for sexist reasons. There is every reason to understand that it is forbidden on moral grounds. The Bible's failure to mention lesbianism specifically is hardly proof that lesbianism was permissible.

Rather, these activities are prohibited because they grow out of and lead to a world view that is radically opposed to that of the Bible.

Adultery, incest, homosexuality and bestiality are not prohibited because they are the incidental practices of Israel's pagan neighbors. They are prohibited because they deny the creation order of God and thus the very nature of God Himself. As such, they are not distinct activities that happen to be grouped together. Rather, they represent one common outlook on sex and the world, that is, the denial of boundaries. This is not to say that someone who engages in one of these practices will necessarily engage in the others. It is only to say that the philosophy behind adultery, incest, homosexuality and bestiality is the same. It is a philosophy that denies transcendence with its teachings of firm boundaries between God and His creation and between various parts of that creation.

# Q

**Doesn't the location of the prohibition of homosexuality in the passages in chapters 17-26 of Leviticus, the so-called holiness code, invalidate it as moral law?**

# A

This argument states that for about 100 years many Old Testament scholars have believed that the legal portions of the Old Testament date, in their present form, to 400 B.C. or later. This would place these portions about one thousand years after Moses. Particularly the book of Leviticus is felt to be an expression of priestly religion after the Exile. The emphasis on sacrifice, ceremonial cleanliness and so forth is thought to support such a view. Therefore the argument states that the prohibitions on homosexual behavior could be the work of priests who came very lately onto the scene and opposed the practice merely because Canaanite priests engaged in it rather than because it was false to the Hebrew moral order.

But even if one grants that Leviticus contains late priestly material—a position it is by no means necessary to take—that does not prove the passage opposes homosexual behavior on merely religious grounds. If the material is late, it still shows a remarkable unity with the rest of the Old Testament where the practices characteristic of paganism are attacked for their world view, not simply because they are non-Israelite. But furthermore, whatever the date of Leviticus and whoever were its transmitters, it contains all the types of legislation discussed above—ceremonial, civil and moral. The prohibition of homosexual behavior is for neither ceremonial nor civil reasons. Direct study of each commandment and its immediate connections reveals that homosexual behavior was seen as a moral offense.

# Q

**The biblical writers call homosexual behavior an "abomination." (The word occurs in both Leviticus 18:22 and 20:13 in the King James Version.) But what does "abomination" mean? Does it simply mean disgusting, as in English, or does it have deeper connotations?**

# A

Two Hebrew words are regularly translated "abomination." They are *shiqquts* and *to'evah*. *Shiqquts* occurs 37 times and seems to have special reference to idols and unclean food.

The remainder of the occurrences of *shiqquts* all refer to idols, where the term is used as a synonym for idol with mocking intent.

*To'evah* occurs much more frequently (125 times) and has a wider range of meaning. It is the word used to describe homosexual behavior in general (Lev. 18:26-31). Kenneth Grayston says abomination refers to "anything repugnant to the true nature of person or thing."[2] To be sure, there are instances where this repugnance is culturally rooted, as in Genesis 43:32, where eating with Semites is said to be an abomination to the Egyptians. But by and large the references are to matters much more deeply rooted in the biblical perception of the world.

Given the fact of a transcendent Creator whose character is not simply a reflection of this world, it becomes possible to say that there are some things that are in keeping with His plan and other things that are not. Unlike adultery and incest, however, homosexuality is singled out in its prohibition as an abomination. Like the prohibition of adultery and incest, the ban on homosexual activity does not relate to ceremonial uncleanness or civil justice. It is moral offense, indicated in part by its carrying the penalty of death. This indicates that the writers saw it as an especially significant denial of the creation order.

# Q

**Does the Old Testament say anything about transvestism, which occasionally accompanies homosexual activity?**

# A

"Unisex"—the idea of blurring or eliminating distinctions between the sexes—is an abomination to God. The statement in Deuteronomy 22:5 that forbids a person to wear the clothing of the other sex has sometimes been used to argue that women should not wear pants. The absurd nature of such an appeal has often obscured the real point. That point is that one should not dress (in whatever style) so as to deny one's sex. It is thus speaking to the "drag queen" and the transvestite and not to evolving styles in clothing. The use of the term "abomination" (KJV) clues us that the command concerns something false to the creation order.

# Q

**Do all scholars agree that the story of Sodom and Gomorrah involves homosexual behavior?**

# A

Only recently has any question been raised about the implications of the account of Sodom and Gomorrah. The church's understanding of it has been uniform for 1,900 years. The word *sodomy* is a fixed part of the English language as a euphemism for homosexual behavior.

Perhaps the first writer to call for the reinterpretation of Genesis 19 was Derrick Bailey in 1954.[3] However, numerous others have followed him since that time. Bailey seems to be of the opinion that this story constitutes the main basis from the Old Testament for prohibiting homosexual behavior and that if the account has been wrongly understood, any rationale for condemning the activity disappears. However, as discussed above, whatever the Sodom and Gomorrah account may say, the teaching of the Torah stands on its own to prohibit homosexual behavior.

# Q

**How do the passages in Genesis 19 and Judges 19 tell the story?**

# A

"But before they lay down, the men of the city, the men of Sodom, both young and old, all the people to the last man, surrounded the house; and they called to Lot, 'Where are the men who came to you tonight? Bring them out to us, that we may know them.' Lot went out of the door to the men, shut the door after him, and said, 'I beg you, my brothers, do not act so wickedly. Behold, I have two daughters who have not known man; let me bring them out to you, and do to them as you please; only do nothing to these men, for they have come under the shelter of my roof.' But they said, 'Stand back!' And they said, 'This fellow came to sojourn, and he would play the judge! Now we will deal worse with you than with them.' Then they pressed hard against the man Lot, and drew near to break the door (Gen. 19:4-9 RSV).

"As they were making their hearts merry, behold, the men of the city, base fellows, beset the house round about, beating on the door; and they said to the old man, the master of the house, 'Bring out the man who came into your house, that we may know him.' And the man, the master of the house, went out to them and said to them, 'No, my brethren, do not act so wickedly; seeing that this man has come into my house, do not do this vile thing. Behold, here are my virgin daughter and his concubine; let me bring them out now. Ravish them and do with them what seems good to you; but against this man do not do so vile a thing.' But the men would not listen to him. So the man seized his concubine, and put her out to them; and they knew her, and abused her all night until the morning. And as the dawn began to

## What arguments do the people who deny the traditional interpretation of the sin of Sodom use?

Briefly, Bailey argues as follows: Neither the Old Testament, nor the Apocrypha, nor the Talmud treat the passage as specifically referring to homosexuality. Only the pseudepigraphists, the Jewish writers Philo and Josephus and the supposedly questionable New Testament books of 2 Peter and Jude do so. Nor do the clear biblical prohibitions of homosexual behavior appeal to the Sodom and Gomorrah (or Gibeah) story for support.

break, they let her go" (Judg. 19:22-25 RSV).

# Q

**Are we sure the word "know" means "to have sexual relations with" in these biblical accounts? Could the men of Sodom have wished merely to meet the stranger?**

# A

Biblical commentators have always understood that *know* here has sexual reference, as it does in Genesis 4:1, for example, and several other places. However, Bailey points out that the word *know* has sexual reference only 14 times out of a total of 943 occurrences. Therefore, he suggests, the odds are against its having a sexual reference here. This interpretation is astonishing. Odds have nothing to do with linguistic usage. Context determines meaning. If the word never had a sexual usage elsewhere, but the etymology permitted it and the context demanded it, that would be enough.

What about the context? First of all, notice that both passages use the word *know* with unmistakable sexual connotations. Genesis 19:8 speaks of "daughters who have not known a man," and Judges 19:25 says, "They knew her, and abused her all night." The context is clearly sexual and suggests strongly that when the inhabitants demanded to know the visitors, they were speaking in sexual terms. If they were merely proposing to get better acquainted with the travelers, as Bailey suggests, the offering of the daughters and the concubine makes no sense.

# Q

**But wouldn't the offering of women have been abhorrent to the men of Sodom if they had been "truly" homosexual?**

# A

The Bible does not say they were "truly" homosexual, whatever that is. It implies from the abusing of the concubine in Judges 19 that they were, in one of today's terms, "kinky." It is simply that for those men sex with males was a little more bizarre and, therefore, desirable. That the intentions were sexual is supported by the fact that both accounts agree that such action would be wicked (Gen. 19:7) or vile (Judg. 19:24). Nor can the deep hostility of the men toward Lot for refusing their demand be, as Bailey suggests, merely pique at Lot's accusing them of inhospitality (an accusation it is hard to see in the text). In short, both contexts suggest very strongly that homosexual "knowledge" is the subject.

# Q

**But, isn't it true that the references to Sodom and Gomorrah in the rest of the Old Testament do not indicate that they were destroyed because their inhabitants were homosexual?**

# A

Neither does Genesis. God had made up His mind to destroy the cities before the homosexual outrage (Gen. 18:20). Why? Because they had gone the full route described in Romans 1. That road begins with pride and leads to idolatry and adultery and homosexuality. In other words, it was a culture gone totally false. To say that it was destroyed because it entertained homosexuality is like saying a dog was destroyed because it bit a child. In fact, the dog was destroyed because it had rabies. The biting was only a symptom.

# Q

**What does a study of Old Testament references to homosexual behavior mean to us today?**

# A

Our options are clear. We may accept the Bible's authority over us or we may deny that authority. If we choose the latter, let us say so. Let us say the Bible does not speak to our age and be done with it. Or, believing the Bible, let us be done with the high-sounding statements that allude to the necessity of advanced training in hermeneutics if one is to understand the "true" import of the text. Such claims simply deny the Bible's plain teaching. Let us accede to it or deny it. But let us not betray it by bending the Bible to support the whims of the pagan culture that surround us.

# 3

# What the New Testament Says About Homosexuality

## J. Harold Greenlee

Recently translations of New Testament references to homosexuality have come into question. Dr. Greenlee deals with this and other challenges to scriptural interpretation.

**Q**

**What is the New Testament's attitude towards sex?**

**A**

The New Testament is neither puritanical nor prudish in its attitudes and teachings about sex. The Old West is sometimes described as the place "where men were men, and women were glad of it!" Within proper limits this quip reflects the New Testament attitude toward sex—a recognition that men and women are distinct, that they are attracted to each other and that they need each other. The New Testament is

*J. Harold Greenlee is a missionary of OMS International and formerly professor of New Testament Greek at Asbury Theological Seminary, Wilmore, Kentucky. He holds the following degrees: A.B., Asbury College, Wilmore, Kentucky; B.D., Asbury Theological Seminary, Wilmore, Kentucky; M.A., University of Kentucky; Ph.D., Harvard University. Dr. Greenlee is the author of several books, including* A Concise Exegetical Grammar of New Testament Greek, An Introduction to New Testament Textual Criticism *and* Scribes, Scrolls, and Scripture. *He has written more than one hundred articles dealing principally with the Greek New Testament for popular and scholarly periodicals. His writings appear in the* Zondervan Pictorial Encyclopedia of the Bible, The Expositor's Bible Commentary *and other works.*

not Victorian in its view of sex or its discussion of it. In the original Greek text it is even less so than in many English translations.

At the same time, the New Testament does not glorify sex nor give it the disproportionate prominence that many aspects of our Western culture insist on doing today. The New Testament treats sex as one important part of life but not as the most important.

## Q

**What role should sex play in our lives, according to the New Testament?**

## A

The New Testament view is that sexual desire is God-given and that it is divinely intended to issue, under proper circumstances, in sexual relations. These proper circumstances for sexual relations are specifically defined: within marriage, between husband and wife and under no other circumstances. No person can read the New Testament in its original language or in the common translations of it with objectivity and come to any other conclusion.

## Q

**Isn't it true that Jesus never condemns homosexuality?**

## A

Yes, but Jesus never said anything in favor of homosexuality either. The burden of proof rests with those who claim that Jesus, in complete opposition to the mores of His Jewish culture, could have approved of homosexual practices.

In Matthew 19:4 Jesus says, "Haven't you read that at the beginning the Creator 'made them male and female'. . . ?" This verse clearly implies that there are two forms of human life, and two only. The emphatic terms male and female (*arsen* and *thelys*) are used here rather than simply man and woman (*aner* and *gyne*). This and the nature of the expression imply exclusiveness of categories—that is, these two and no other forms.

Jesus then quotes Genesis 2:24 as further support of this idea of male-female exclusiveness: "For this reason a man will leave his father and mother and be united to his wife, and the two will become one flesh. . . .So they are no longer two, but one" (Matthew 19:5-6).

## Q

**Why is there no mention of**

**possible same-sex unions here?**

# A

Jesus could have stated, had He wished to do so, that the principle of a husband's becoming joined to his wife applied also to two persons of the same sex in a sexual union. After all, Jesus felt free to modify the interpretation of some points of the Old Testament in words such as "You have heard... But I tell you ..." (Matt. 5:21-22). If some persons are "born" homosexuals and their homosexual behavior is thus a valid lifestyle, Jesus at this point might have referred to homosexuals and indicated His acceptance of their natural condition and needs. He could have added some statement such as, "And I say to you that when a man becomes joined to any other man, or a woman to another woman, they likewise become one flesh." If Jesus accepted the validity of homosexuality, somewhere in the Gospels He ought to have indicated His disagreement with the Old Testament's condemnation of homosexual behavior (see Leviticus 20:13 and chapter two of this book).

The plain fact is that neither here nor anywhere else in the Gospels does Jesus give the slightest basis for assuming that He considered homosexual unions, much less promiscuous homosexual behavior, to be an acceptable lifestyle. Nor may we suppose that He was ignorant of homosexuality. Even if we overlook the Old Testament references, homosexuality was well known in the world of Jesus' day, although it was far less common among the Jews than among the Greeks and Romans.

# Q

**Does Jesus approve of sexual relationships other than male-female marriage?**

# A

Jesus does, indeed, recognize one possible alternative to marriage: viz., celibacy— whether voluntary or because of sterility at birth or by emasculation (Matt. 19:11-12). The only reasonable conclusion to draw from the Gospels is that Jesus considered the only legitimate sexual relationship to be between one man and one woman in a permanent union.

# Q

**Does the New Testament indicate that Jesus despises homosexuals?**

# A

No. Homosexuals were surely included in Jesus' circle of love. Jesus was no religious legalist, and some of His harshest condemnations were for those who were. He flatly told a group of Jewish priests and religious leaders, "Truly I say to you that the tax collectors and the prostitutes will enter the kingdom of God ahead of you" (Matt. 21:31, author's translation). The story of the woman taken in adultery likewise shows Jesus' love for a person who was guilty of sexual sin (John 7:53-8:11).[1] Yet in neither of these instances is there any hint that Jesus' love for a person includes condoning of sexual sin. To the woman taken in adultery He said, "Go now and leave your life of sin" (8:11).

# Q

**Doesn't *agape* (the most common Greek word for "love" in the New Testament, referring to a recognition of the infinite value of a person) demand that we accept homosexuals?**

# A

There is much confusion concerning *agape* love, as if this acceptance of the person were the end of the matter. It is not. God does accept each of us as a person, without regard to our virtues or faults. He accepts us, however, with the full intention of changing us from what we are to what we ought to be. Hebrews says: "The Lord disciplines those he loves. . . Endure hardship as discipline; God is treating you as sons. . . God disciplines us for our good, that we may share in his holiness" (12:6-10). Paul says, "For he [God] chose us in him [Christ] before the creation of the world to be holy and blameless in his sight" (Eph. 1:4).

Contrast this with the statement of a United Methodist minister, John V. Moore:

Understanding God as the Word who came and dwelt among foolish and fragile mortals, I could not be intimidated to refrain from relating with people who were different from myself. I was enabled to receive in a new way God's treasures which always come to us in earthen vessels.[2]

There is no seeking of the best interest of the person, in this case the homosexual, but merely acceptance. *Agape* love accepts the alcoholic, the proud, the sexually immoral, the person filled with hatred or overwhelmed with an inferiority complex; but any attitude that is content to leave these persons in such conditions is not the *agape* love with which God loves us and with which He calls us to love each other.

## Q

**Isn't it unfair for heterosexuals to insist that homosexuals change their sexual orientation?**

## A

Moore raises this question of the difficulty of a homosexual person changing his or her behavior. He says,

> As I reflect upon the demand that those who are homosexual change their orientation, I wondered how I might respond to a similar demand. For more than twenty years Barbara and I had gone to bed every night in the same four-poster. For a judge or a preacher or counselor to demand that I change my sexual identification struck me as absurd. For the police and my fellow citizens to put me in jail or deprive me of my job, I could regard only as unjust and cruel.[3]

Moore's comment ignores the question as to whether homosexual behavior is or is not in violation of the Scriptures. He attempts to equate insisting that a person cease illegitimate sexual behavior with insisting that a person cease *legitimate* sexual behavior. This is like saying, "I cannot insist that one man should stop robbing banks to earn his living because I would not want someone to insist that I stop operating my grocery store to earn my living"!

Some maintain that homosexual behavior is acceptable to God, and that the homosexual person can, with God's approval and a clear conscience, continue in homosexual behavior. However, the claim that God accepts a person even though he or she is a homosexual implies that God is willing for a person to continue homosexual behavior. This claim overlooks the fact that God's acceptance of a person has nothing to do with either that person's virtues or vices. God accepts us with the full intention of not leaving us as He finds us but of making us like Himself, causing us to partake of the quality of holiness that is His own central characteristic.

# Q

**Does the New Testament specifically prohibit a loving homosexual relationship?**

# A

The New Testament teaches that sexual relations are God's will for a husband and wife, to be carried out solely within marriage. Sex is an expression of love and unity between husband and wife and the means of preserving the family and propagating the race.

If it is true that sexual relations are exclusively for a husband and his wife, then all sexual acts outside of marriage are condemned. All homosexual acts fail to fulfill the purposes for which sex was created.

# Q

**Although the New Testament doesn't mention same-sex marriage, couldn't homosexual experiences still be permissible as long as they are loving?**

# A

The New Testament teaching sharply contrasts with statements such as those of Troy Perry: "I believe that there can be loving experiences, even in a one-night stand. I truly believe that two individuals can meet and share their complete beings with each other, totally sexually too, and never see each other again; and remember it as a beautiful, loving situation."[4] If such promiscuous homosexual one-night stands would have God's approval, then surely He would approve of similar heterosexual encounters. But these God condemns as fornication and adultery! How then can we presume to claim God's approval of such activity in a homosexual relationship? If there is no room in Jesus' teaching for some type of a permanent homosexual union analogous to marriage, then it is sheer desperation to try to claim His approval of a homosexual action apart from any such union.

# Q

**How does homosexuality relate to promiscuous or extramarital heterosexual relations?**

# A

Advocates of homosexual behavior as a legitimate lifestyle overlook one logical prerequisite: namely, that extramarital and promiscuous heterosexual behavior must be shown to be legitimate before the legitimacy of homosexual behavior should be discussed. Homosexual behavior is commonly casual and promiscuous. Only infrequently does it result in a permanent relationship. The Christian standard demands that there be no sexual relations prior to or outside of marriage. It is rare to find a homosexual couple in a settled relationship who had no sexual relations with anyone before or after establishing their union. Nor do most defenders of homosexual behavior argue to legitimize only settled relationships. They do not reject promiscuous homosexual behavior. Instead they argue for their right to casual relationships. What they insist on is complete freedom for any type of same-sex acts and behavior, without restraint.

# Q

**Even though the Bible condemns promiscuous sexual behavior, whether homosexual or heterosexual, does it forbid monogamous homosexual relationships?**

# A

First Corinthians 7:1 states, "It is good for a man not to marry." Paul is stating that celibacy is a legitimate option for those who feel led in this direction. He continues, however, by stating that the safer course is marriage: "But since there is so much immorality, each man should have his own wife, and each woman her own husband" (v. 2).

The Greek word *aner* used in 1 Corinthians 7:2 means both "man" and "husband," and the Greek word *gyne* means both "woman" and "wife." Thus, in this and similar passages the language leaves no room for a same-sex union; such a relationship would have to be expressed in other words, such as *anthropos*, the more common word for "man," which is a generic word that can also mean "person" without emphasis on gender.

This passage cannot mean, "Let each man have his own wife or male bed-companion (*koinolektros*) and each woman have her own husband or female bed-companion." Why does he not admit the additional option of a homosexual union? Such relations were well known and practiced in Corinth and they probably could more readily have been made respectable in the Christian community of Corinth

# Could Paul Be Wrong?

What Paul says in these passages expresses God's inspired Word. This point is worth making, since some advocates of free homosexual behavior treat the apostle's opinions on homosexuality as being subject to correction. For example, John V. Moore states, "I am still persuaded that Paul condemned homosexual acts. I disagree with his understanding of them simply as perverse choices. . . . His judgments did not absolve me from taking seriously the findings of contemporary researchers, nor my own experience."[5] Moore's conclusion is clearly that the judgments of Scripture may be amended by the conclusions of present-day authorities.

It is true that Paul sometimes speaks to a local situation. When he does so, his directions may or may not apply to our own culture and situation. But even in these passages his words were written under the inspiration of the Holy Spirit and contain principles of value to our lives. In the passages referring to homosexuality I find no factors that disqualify his words from general application.

Someone may question Paul's comments in 1 Corinthians 7:12: "To the rest I say this (I, not the Lord). . . ." But here he means that he does not have a specific word from Jesus' earthly ministry to which he can refer the Corinthians, as he did in verse 10: "I give this command (not I, but the Lord). . . ."

In verses 25-26 he states, "Now about virgins: I have no command from the Lord, but I give a judgment as one who by the Lord's mercy is trustworthy. . . .I think that. . . ." Here too, Paul does not mean he is speaking merely from his own human understanding; he means that he has no specific commandment from the lips of Jesus. Therefore, as *The Expositor's Greek New Testament* explains, he is dealing here with "conditional advice" rather than a "peremptory rule."[6] In verse 40 he gives the qualification, "In my judgment. . .and I think that I too have the Spirit of God."

Here again he is giving advice, not a command, hence the "judgment." As for thinking that he has the Spirit of God, to quote *Expositor's Greek New Testament* again, "It is the language of modesty, not of misgiving. The Apostle commends his advice in all these matters, conscious that it proceeds from the highest source and is not the outcome of mere human prudence or personal inclination."[7] Therefore, this passage as well as all of Paul's letters are the authoritative and binding Word of God.

than in many other localities. If mere avoidance of sexual promiscuity were Paul's concern, a settled homosexual union would have served that purpose as well as heterosexual marriage. It is clear then that Paul did not consider a homosexual union a legitimate choice for a Christian.

## Q

**Does Paul mention any options for Christians besides male-female marriage or celibacy?**

## A

In 1 Corinthians 7:25-40 Paul discusses some problems of the married and the unmarried or widows. He goes into some detail in giving advice and expressing his concern. Once again we should remind ourselves that homosexuality was common in Corinth and in the Roman world in general. William Barclay, a well-known New Testament scholar, notes that Greek society was thoroughly permeated with homosexuality. But even though it was nearly universal, "it was regarded as abnormal, and it was never legal."[8] Yet in the whole of 1 Corinthians 7 Paul gives no hint that the Corinthian Christians might

engage in homosexual activity or homosexual unions as alternatives to, or in addition to, either marriage or celibacy. Verse 39 says that if a woman's husband dies, "she is free to marry anyone she wishes, but he must belong to the Lord."

This permission does not include a possible lesbian relationship with another woman. Since Paul has nowhere given any indication that he considers a same-sex union to be permissible for Christians, no reasonable exegesis will permit the masculine pronoun "whom" here to include another woman.

## Q

**Can't husband-wife roles be filled by participants in a homosexual relationship?**

## A

Ephesians 5:22-33 discusses an exclusively husband-wife relationship. Paul points out that the wife should be subject to (this is not equivalent to being dominated by) her husband and that the husband should love his wife with *agape* love. He also adds the familiar reference from Genesis 2:24. If homosexual unions were proper, why did Paul not include such relationships in these exhortations?

We cannot assume that the principles Paul expresses in Ephesians 5:22-33 can tacitly be extrapolated to apply to homosexual unions. He nowhere gives any grounds for supposing that he includes homosexual unions in his thoughts on marriage relationships. In addition, the husband-wife roles and responsibilities as described here would not apply to a same-sex union; that would require a different orientation of roles.

Jesus declares that the joining of a husband and wife, the male with the female, produces a unity in which the male and the female are no longer two but one flesh. Each of the two was, in a sense, a half. The explicit phrase *male and female* suggests that these are not identical but complementary halves. Genesis 2:18 does not say that God decided to create an identical twin for Adam but a "helper suitable for him," a complementary person. The union is not like the two halves of a circle. A better analogy is a pair of shoes. A union of two females or two males does not make a united whole but rather a repetition of identical halves. The result compares to a "pair" of two left-foot shoes or a person with a right hand on each arm.

# Q

**Should practicing homosexuals hold leadership positions in the church?**

# A

Paul states that an *episkopos* ("overseer"), a *diakonos* ("deacon") and a *presbyteros* ("elder") must be the "husband of one wife" (1 Tim. 3:2,12, cf. Titus 1:6). While there are differences in interpretation of this phrase, it certainly prohibits sexual immorality. It means that a man must be true to his wife. The assumption is that he will usually be a married man, but there is no intention of disqualifying a bachelor, a widower or a remarried widower if his moral life is proper. However, "husband" and "wife" are specifically "man" (*aner*) and "woman" (*gyne*)—designations that could hardly be extended to include a same-sex union. The obvious conclusion is that these church officials were not permitted to engage in homosexual actions.

This argument is strengthened by a reference to 1 Timothy 5:9, which states that a widow, to be enrolled for aid from the church, must have been "the wife of one husband"(RSV). Again neither explicitly nor implicitly is there any basis for assuming that a lesbian partner would be considered an acceptable alternative to a husband. The idea that homosexual activities were not mentioned in these passages merely because they were of no moral significance is simply inconceivable.

## Q

**Were the New Testament writers ignorant of homosexuality? This could explain why they don't mention homosexual relations in passages about marriage.**

## A

New Testament authors could not have been ignorant of something so common as homosexuality in the Greco-Roman world. They could hardly have remained silent because of unconcern; in such a case they would certainly have stated that homosexuality was of no moral significance. And we have no reason to assume that *gamos* ("marriage") could have been understood by their readers to include a same-sex union.

Jude 7 states that "Sodom and Gomorrah and the sur-rounding towns who gave themselves up to sexual immorality and went after other flesh serve as an example of those who suffer the punishment of eternal fire"(author's translation). What "went after other flesh" means is clear from the story of the angels' deliverance of Lot and his family from the city of Sodom, which along with the other cities of the plain, was destroyed by fire from God. They were guilty of homosexuality (see chapter two), and the New Testament writers knew this.

## Q

**Isn't it true that the word "homosexual" did not appear until the 1880s—the Victorian era? Perhaps people in New Testament times simply didn't have our hangups about homosexuality.**

## A

In the New Testament the principle word for same-sex activities is *arsenokoites* (in older Greek, *arrenokoites*). This word is found in the Sibylline Oracles and Diogenes Laertius, which means it is as old as the New Testament. We may doubt the objective scholarship of a clergyman such as John

Boswell who has stated that the word homosexual was not coined until the 1880s and that "ancient people did not distinguish between" homosexual and heterosexual persons. "Sexuality was sexuality," he declares.[9]

As to precisely when the English word "homosexual" originated, Boswell may be correct. But the ancient Greeks and Romans did not speak English! To take a supposed late date for this particular English word and conclude that the idea of homosexuality was unknown or undistinguished from heterosexual behavior in earlier times is simply absurd. Even the 1611 King James Version of the Bible contradicts Boswell's claim. It translates the specific word for male homosexuality, *arsenokoites*, as "abusers of themselves with mankind" in 1 Corinthians 6:9 and as "them that defile themselves with mankind" in 1 Timothy 1:10. These phrases may seem obscure to us, but the very use of these euphemisms for homosexuality, when heterosexual sins are described with explicit terms (adultery, fornication, whoremonger and harlot) shows that the translators knew perfectly well what the

term meant but they considered it so much more degraded than adultery that they refused to name it specifically.

Matthew Poole published his *Annotations on the Holy Bible* in 1685. In regard to Romans 1:26 he says, "If they. . .that commit fornication dishonour their own bodies, then much more do they that practice the unnatural uncleanness hereafter mentioned." He goes on to refer to the homosexual acts mentioned here as "a filthy practice not to be named," although he did not hesitate to name fornication. In 1 Corinthians 6:9 he refers to the word for male homosexuality as describing "the sin of Sodom, a sin not to be named among Christians or men." Concerning the words *fornicators* (which here may mean immoral persons generally) and *male homosexuals*, he says, "[These] two terms express violations of the seventh commandment, whether by fornication, adultery, incest, sodomy, or any beastly lusts."[10]

## Q

**Does this sound as if Poole could not distinguish between heterosexual and homosexual sin?**

# A

John Albert Bengel's commentary, *Gnomon of the New Testament*, was first published in Latin in 1742 and was translated into English about 1857. In the discussion of the homosexual degradation described in Romans 1:26-27, Bengel uses no more specific words than "burned with an abominable fire. . .viz., of lust" and "that which is unseemly, against which the conformation of the body and its members [recoils]." In 1 Corinthians 6:9 he refers to homosexual behavior vaguely as "scandalous crimes," and in 1 Timothy 1:10 he passes over this same word.[11] S.T. Bloomfield, in his commentary of 1839, likewise avoids frank terms. Referring in Romans 1:26-27, he writes about "the dreadful corruption of morals in the ancient world." He also avoids a direct reference to "homosexuals" in 1 Corinthians 6:9 and 1 Timothy 1:10.[12.]

# Q

**Does this avoidance of explicit terms mean that these seventeenth- to nineteenth-century authors did not know what homosexuality was or that they made no distinction between homosexual and heterosexual acts, as Dr. Boswell implies?**

# A

On the contrary, these same writers have no hesitancy to use the words *fornication* and *adultery* and to point out the difference between these two terms where they find it appropriate. Their lack of frankness with reference to homosexual acts is due to the fact that they regarded these acts as so much more abominable and shameful than even adultery and fornication that they were reluctant to name them.

# Q

**Was the issue of homosexuality discussed by church leaders during the centuries between the writing of the New Testament and today?**

# A

Homosexuality was indeed known and abhorred between the first centuries and today.

Thomas Aquinas, who lived from 1224 to 1274, refers in his *Summa Theologica* to the "unnatural vice," including under this heading "autoeroticism" (which he calls "effeminacy"), "bestiality" and "sodomy" (under the latter he includes both male and female homosexuality). He further comments, "In every genus, worst of all is the corruption of the principle on which the rest depend. . . Therefore, since by the unnatural vices man transgresses that which has been determined by nature with regard to the use of venereal [sexual] actions, it follows that in this matter this sin is gravest of all. After it comes incest." Further on, he says that in these homosexual acts, which are "sins contrary to nature, whereby the very order of nature is violated, an injury is done to God, the Author of nature."[13] Bridging the period between Aquinas and the New Testament, in the same discussion on homosexual sins Aquinas refers to Augustine (A.D. 354-430), stating, "Hence Augustine says (Confessions iii. 8): 'Those foul offenses that are against nature should be everywhere and at all times detested and punished, such as were those of the people of Sodom.'"[14]

This does not indicate that people in past centuries "did not distinguish between" heterosexual and homosexual actions and sins. Rather, it reveals that certain apologists for homosexual license are shutting their eyes to disagreeable data.

**Q**

**What is the exact meaning of the Greek word *arsenokoites* mentioned earlier? Could it have been mistranslated?**

**A**

To return to the Greek word under discussion, *arsenokoites*, Thayer's Greek-English Lexicon (1885) renders this word as "one who lies with a male as with a female, a sodomite." The more recent edition of Bauer, Arndt and Gingrich's lexicon (1957) translates it as "a male homosexual, pederast, sodomite," citing this meaning in the ancient *Anthologia Palatina*, the *Catalogus Codicum Astrologorum Graecorum* and the related verb from the *Sibylline Oracles*.

There is no doubt concerning the meaning of *arsenokoites*. It is derived from *arsen* (in older Greek, *arren*) ("a male") and *koite* ("a bed"). With the suffix -*tes* indicating the agent of an action, the etymology of the word is "a male-bed-person." The word *arsen* puts emphasis on the aspect of gender or sex, in distinction both from *aner* ("man" as distinct from woman) and *anthropos* ("man" or person generically). The second part of this word, *koite*, is the ordinary word for "bed" (as in Luke 11:7, "my children are with me in bed"). From this primary sense the meaning is extended to the marriage bed (as in Hebrews 13:4, "The marriage bed kept pure"). The idiom "to have a bed" means to become pregnant, as in Romans 9:10; and the plural (beds) has the meaning of sexual excesses in Romans 13:13.

It is clear, then, that an *arsenokoites* in the New Testament is a man who goes to bed with a male for sexual purposes. This has been its accepted meaning ever since the time of ancient Greek literature. Even though only the one person, the male, is mentioned in this word, it has always been understood to mean male-with-male; it has never had the implication of a male going to bed with a female. To state therefore, as does Boswell, that Paul's condemnations of homosexuality in the English New Testament are "blatant mistranslations," and "I doubt that Paul had any concept of homosexuality as a separate category of human beings," is inexcusable ignorance or worse.[15] The fact is that an ancient Greek reading the New Testament for the first time, with no previous knowledge of Christian moral standards, would have not the slightest difficulty in understanding the meaning of *arsenokoites*.

# Q

**Are any other Greek words relating specifically to homosexuality used in the New Testament?**

# A

A second word relevant to our discussion is *malakos*. The basic meaning of this word is "soft"; it is used in Matthew 11:8 and Luke 7:25 in a neutral sense of "soft clothing, such as fastidious people wear" (Bauer, Arndt and Gingrich, *Greek-English Lexicon of the New Testament*). The same lexicon gives *malakos* the further meaning of "soft, effeminate, especially of catamites," the term *catamite* being defined as "men and boys who allow themselves to be misused sexually." The lexicon cites instances of this meaning of the word from the *Hibeh Papyri* of the late B.C. and early A.D. period and from the writings of Dionysius of Halicarnassus, Dio Chrysostom, Vettius Valens and Diogenes Laertius of the first three

Christian centuries.

*Malakos* in this moral sense is found in 1 Corinthians 6, along with other words denoting sexual immorality: "Do you not know that the wicked will not inherit the kingdom of God? Do not be deceived: Neither the sexually immoral [*pornoi*] nor idolaters nor adulterers [*moichoi*] nor male prostitutes [*malakoi*] nor homosexual offenders [*arsenokoitai*] nor thieves nor the greedy. . .will inherit the kingdom of God. And that is what some of you were. But you were washed, you were sanctified, you were justified in the name of the Lord Jesus Christ and by the Spirit of our God" (vv. 9-11).

This Scripture could hardly have stated more clearly that the Christians who had been guilty of homosexual behavior—as well as those who had been guilty of heterosexual sins, stealing, drunkenness and other sins—had been delivered by repentance and faith in Jesus Christ. The apostle says the believers were "washed. . . sanctified. . .justified." They no longer engaged in these sins; Paul says "you were," not "you are."

**Q**

**Isn't it possible for heterosexuals to sin against each other, even in marriage?**

**A**

We cannot avoid the weight of Paul's condemnation of homosexual acts by dragging out the red herring that it is possible to sin against one's own spouse through misuse of sex within the marriage bond. Some husbands and wives doubtless do sin against each other and against God by the misuse of sexual relations with each other. However, just as the fact that some persons have been harmed by misuse of water is no argument in favor of alcohol, so instances of misuse of heterosexual relations do not alleviate the sinfulness of homosexual acts.

**Q**

**Isn't the New Testament vague when referring to homosexuality?**

**A**

Neither an ancient Greek nor a modern scholar of the Greek language would have the slightest difficulty in understanding Paul's clear and obvious meaning in Romans 1:24-27 when he states, "Therefore God gave them over in the sinful desires of their hearts to uncleanness [akatharsia] in order to dishonor their bodies with one another. . . .Because of this, God gave them over to passions of dishonor. For [both of the following things occurred (Gk. te)] their females [theleiai] exchanged natural [physiken] relations for unnatural ones. In the same way the males [arsenes] also abandoned natural relations with females and were inflamed with lust [orexis] for one another. Males committed indecent acts with males, and received in themselves the due penalty for their perversion"(author's translation). Then, following a further list of sins of various types, he summarizes the degradation of these sinners by saying, "Although they know God's righteous decree [dikaioma] that those who do such things deserve death, they not only continue to do these very things but also approve of those who practice them" (v. 32). How much more plainly could the Bible have declared that these men and women became involved in homosexual desires and behavior, and that such things, as well as other sins that are mentioned, are willful violations of the known will of God and are deserving of the punishment of death!

*Arsenokoites* appears again in the New Testament in 1 Timothy 1:9-10 (author's translation): "We also know that law is made not for good men but for lawbreakers and rebels, the ungodly and sinful, the unholy and irreligious; for those who kill their fathers or mothers, for murderers, for adulterers [pornoi] and male homosexuals [arsenokoitai], for slave traders and liars and oath-breakers—and for whatever else is contrary to the sound doctrine." To pretend that one of the actions involved in this dreary list—homosexuality—is not always wrong and sinful and that it may indeed be perfectly acceptable behavior for a Christian is simply to call clean what the New Testament calls unclean.

# Q

**Does the New Testament condemn homosexuals, or only homosexual actions?**

# A

To say that the New Testament condemns homosexual actions is not to say that it explicitly condemns homosexuality as a personal tendency. When we use the term *homosexuality* in a context of condemnation, we are referring to homosexual behavior and not to homosexual tendencies. It is not within the province of this chapter to deal with the origin of homosexual tendencies. However, it would certainly be inconsistent with the righteous character of the God who is revealed to us in the New Testament to condemn what is simply the natural behavior of a person as created by God. Nevertheless both the New Testament's presentation of an exclusively male-female concept of sexuality and its categorical condemnation of homosexual behavior every time such behavior is mentioned clearly imply that homosexuality is not, like heterosexuality, a gift of God.

## Q

**If the New Testament doesn't condemn a person for having homosexual tendencies, how can a person who acts on those innate tendencies be blamed for his or her actions?**

## A

Let us suppose, for argument's sake, that it can be proven that some persons have a "natural" tendency toward homosexuality. Even this would not prove that homosexuality is created by God and is therefore a lifestyle acceptable to Him. Consider the universal tendency toward sin in general, from which no person is free in his natural condition. Shall we pronounce this condition God-given and declare that a life of sinning is therefore a divinely approved way of life for the Christian?

Following such reasoning should we not help the alcoholic secure enough alcohol to satisfy his "natural" desire? Should we not help the kleptomaniac satisfy his proclivity to stealing and the psychotic killer his compulsion to kill?

We should not be surprised if the condition in which we are born differs from the condition in which man was created by God. Genesis 2-3 describe a well-known incident in the Garden of Eden that distorted God's image, not only in our first parents but in all their descendants as well. From that moment until the present it has been more "natural" for human beings to sin than to live in holiness. But this neither excuses nor legitimizes even one person's yielding to this sinful nature and continuing in a life of sin.

As a part of the resultant depravity in the human heart and mind—a depravity that infected every area of life—the sexual aspect was distorted. This beautiful gift of God for husband and wife became twisted to include Satan's parodies of sex—fornication, adultery, homosexuality, autoeroticism, bestiality and other aberrations.

# Q

**Does the New Testament say a person with homosexual tendencies sins by merely desiring to commit homosexual acts?**

# A

Whatever the origin of homosexual tendencies, the New Testament condemns homosexual *actions*. This condemnation extends to the desire to commit the act (as distinct from mere temptation), just as the desire to commit adultery is condemned as the equivalent of the adulterous act (Matthew 5:27-28). This means that a person with homosexual tendencies is expected to resist the temptation to homosexual activity by the help of the Holy Spirit, just as an unmarried person is expected to resist the temptation to commit fornication and as a married person is expected to resist the temptation to commit adultery.

If a person fails to resist the temptation that comes to him and commits sin—be it homosexual, heterosexual or any other type of sin—God's grace offers him the opportunity to repent and be forgiven. 1 John 2:1-2 assures us, "If anyone does sin, we have an advocate with the Father, Jesus Christ, the Righteous One. He is the expiation for our sins" (author's translation).

# Q

**Isn't it unfair to demand that homosexuals deny their natural inclination to engage in homosexual acts?**

# A

To expect a person, with divine help, to resist homosexual tendencies is not the harsh and unequal treatment some defenders of homosexuality claim. Heterosexually-oriented persons are likewise commanded by the New Testament to refrain from sexual actions, both in thought and deed, except within the marriage bond. All of us know that many persons, both men and women, including some who make no claim to be Christians, go through life without sexual experience and that many married persons who are separated from their spouses for periods of time can and do keep themselves free from sexual involvement during those times. Yet how many of these people have not been subjected to sexual temptation and even sexual opportunity? If there is victory over heterosexual temptations, especially with the divine resources available to the Christian, then victory is surely possible over tendencies to homosexual sins as well. This is the promise of 1 Corinthians 10:13, "No temptation has seized you except what is common to man. And God is faithful; he will not let you be tempted beyond what you can bear, but with the temptation he will also provide the way out so that you can stand up under it" (author's translation).

This struggle with homosexual tendencies is well presented in a book entitled *The Returns of Love*. It is a collection of anonymous letters by a Christian young man who has homosexual tendencies. With divine help he resists these tendencies and seeks to bring himself to a normal heterosexual life. At one point he writes that a homosexual cannot plead before God, "I couldn't help it," because "somewhere along the line his passive submission to sin must

have been a matter of active choice, and for that action he is held responsible."[16]

# Q

**In Galatians 3:28 doesn't Paul support the obliteration of sex distinctions for Christians?**

# A

No. Paul is simply arguing that persons are equal in Christ's sight and that no one is preferred above nor debased below another—neither Jew nor Greek, slave nor free, male nor female. The distinct classes and identities obviously remain, but they are not to be made the basis of privilege or lack of privilege in Christ.

# Q

**Why do people often seek sexual satisfaction outside of marriage?**

# A

The pressure for the satisfaction of the sexual appetite without regard to marriage comes, in large measure, from the sexual stimulation to which many people permit themselves to be subjected. There are also the stimuli that are thrust on them unwittingly—in print, in the theater, on television, by others' immodest dress and in other ways. The stimulation naturally leads to a desire for satisfaction, just as the aroma of a broiling steak stimulates the desire for food in a person who has not eaten for several hours.

The New Testament speaks to this point as well. Warning us against permitting ourselves to be sexually stimulated to a point where sexual desire is aroused, Jesus states that not only is the act of adultery sinful, but "anyone who looks at a woman lustfully has already committed adultery with her in his heart" (Matt. 5:28).

## Q

**Doesn't everyone have the right to sexual fulfillment, even homosexuals?**

## A

If we accept the unbiblical premise that every person is entitled to sexual activity, then it may appear to follow reasonably that if a person's inclinations are homosexual, he or she has the right to homosexual activity. This line of argument clearly implies that the desire and the inclination legitimize the expression. But if this is true then not only homosexual behavior is legitimate but also fornication, adultery and bestiality. This argument may make good humanism, with man the measure of all things. But it is a far cry from the biblical standard of holiness and purity based on the admonition, "Be holy, because I, the Lord your God, am holy" (Lev. 19:2).

Nevertheless, this assumption is commonly presented as valid. Even professing Christians begin to feel that chastity is a losing battle and biblical standards are too idealistic to be maintained or are even irrelevant.

The liberationists' declaration, however, is the Big Lie. The Bible insists on a standard of sexual morality that can be maintained. Countless multitudes have maintained it through the ages and still do, including people of diverse cultures and many who have never heard of the Bible's teachings.

## Q

**Why can't I do as I please with my body?**

## A

Does a person have the right to do as he wishes with his own body? The biblical reply is no. The non-Christian reply might seem to be yes, but even the non-Christian can really go no further than a qualified "Yes, but. . . ."

To illustrate this principle, suppose a man buys a new Cadillac and pays the full price in cash. He drives his luxury car home and finds the owner's manual in the glove compartment. He begins to read the instructions, becomes indignant and says to himself, "This is my car, and General Motors can't tell me what I can and can't do with it!" He then proceeds to do as he pleases with his new car. He decides to put water in the crankcase instead of motor oil. He drives his car through his farmland, hitting boulders and running through ditches. He refuses to check the air pressure in the tires.

General Motors has no legal right to interfere with this mistreatment of a fine car. The owner handles his car as he chooses. However, he cannot avoid the consequences of his choice, which is the ruin of his automobile.

Similarly, we can do as we please with our bodies; God has given us that privilege. However, we must also accept the consequences of our choices. The consequences are

a part of the cause-and-effect relationships of the universe, as implied in passages such as Romans 1:27.

Q

**Why do Christians want to follow the New Testament's rules about sexual conduct?**

A

The Christian says, "I do not have the unrestricted right to do as I please with my body." This response is based on the biblical principle of stewardship, as outlined in 1 Corinthians 6:19-20: "Do you not know that your body is a temple of the Holy Spirit, who is in you, whom you have received from God? You are not your own; you were bought at a price. Therefore honor God with your body."

It is God who "from one man . . . made every nation of men" (Acts 17:26) and "from whom the whole family in heaven and on earth derives its name" (Eph. 3:15). The biblical viewpoint is that God has a right to expect us to care for our bodies in accordance with His commands because we belong to Him. In addition, however, we ought to obey His instructions about the care of our minds and bodies because He created us and best knows how we should live.

In short, we ought to live according to certain principles because these principles correspond to the nature of the real world and because they represent the Creator's will for us. These principles are given to us in the Bible, and they are both correct and a moral obligation to us.

Even the non-Christian who believes in God as Creator should logically assume that if God has given guidelines for life, everyone would be wise to follow those guidelines. The person who rejects the idea of God has no sure guidelines for his life and may therefore grasp at all sorts of substitutes for the "owner's manual."

# Q

**How can our bodies be our own if God dictates how we should live?**

# A

Accepting God's laws as both correct and morally binding, Christians believe that there are some things they have no right to do with their bodies and that there are things two persons have no right to do together even if they are mutually willing. This principle of dual ownership should not be regarded as an anomaly. For example, under our laws a person can be charged with arson if he burns down his own house, even if it is fully paid for and he has no insurance benefits to claim. A farmer on the northern Minnesota border has no legal right to secede from the United States and give his farm to Canada.

In a similar and profound way, God has a claim on us and our bodies—a claim we cannot ultimately avoid. His laws, moreover, are not the mere whims of an arbitrary dictator; they are the principles on which the universe was created and on which it operates. A person who says with the Psalmist, "To do your will, O my God, is my desire," is living in accordance with the nature of things and in obedience to a God of absolute love and perfect holiness who could never want anything less than the best for His children.

# Civil Rights Controversies On Homosexuality

## By Roger J. Magnuson

Homosexuals have been clamoring for legislation prohibiting discrimination based on sexual and affectional preferences. If passed such legislation would have profound influence on the church and society in general.

**Q**

**Why is homosexuality considered a civil rights issue?**

**A**

That efforts to promote acceptance of sexually deviant conduct are perceived as a movement for "civil rights" is a tribute to the political ingenuity of gay rights activists. The tactics are obvious. Homosexuals prefer to frame the issue as one of restoring their "rights," or forbidding "discrimination" against them. By attempting to harness the social momentum generated by successful campaigns for protection of ethnic and religious minorities, homosexuals have hitched their political destiny to a powerful engine.

**Q**

**When did homosexuals begin demanding civil rights?**

**A**

The history of civil rights activ-

***Roger J. Magnuson*** *is a trial lawyer in Minneapolis, Minnesota. An honors graduate of Stanford University, Harvard Law School and Oxford University, he is listed in Who's Who in American Law and is the author of a three volume legal treatise. He has recently written a book on civil rights,* Are Gay Rights Right? *(Straitgate Press, 220 W. 66th Street, Suite 190, Minneapolis, MN 55423).*

ism for homosexuals begins with the riot at the Stonewall Bar in Greenwich Village in June, 1969.

## Q

**Did homosexuals organize prior to the Stonewall Bar incident?**

## A

Before the radically energized 1960s, homosexual behavior was generally furtive. When they exited the closet their steps were tentative, often self-deprecating. In 1948, for example, a "Bachelors for Wallace" group spoke of organizing those who had "our physiological and psychological handicaps . . . toward the constructive social progress of mankind."[1]

During the 1950s groups like the Mattachine Society and the Daughters of Bilitis (for male homosexuals and lesbians, respectively) emerged, but they produced only mimeographed rivulets far from the mainstream of American political discussion.[2] When policemen descended on the Stonewall Bar that June evening in 1969, they found the behavior one would expect at a homosexual bar. They began making arrests.

But this time the homosexuals were not docile. They began to riot. The riot grew into a large parade through Greenwich Village. For the first time hundreds of homosexuals marched publicly in protest. The Stonewall riot ignited an explosion of homosexual activism celebrated in many communities around the country as "gay rights" day.

## Q

**How did the gay rights movement change after the Stonewall demonstration?**

## A

For homosexual activists, the riot marked a critical turning point in strategy and tactics. The strategy was marked by a new "willingness to demand not just tolerance but total acceptance, and by a new militance in making these demands."[3]

The tactics became fixed as well: The homosexual rights movement positions itself as a minority and uses the language and legal precedents of other civil rights campaigns to achieve this "acceptance" of its lifestyle.

## Q

**What hurdles did the fledg-**

ling gay rights movement have to clear to gain popular acceptance?

## A

The homosexuals had to clear two hurdles. One related to language, the other to law.

Words used to describe homosexuals or their conduct had a bad connotation. Words like "sodomy," or the English equivalent "buggery," are well established in the law but do not make persuasive slogans (who would support "buggers' rights" or "sodomites' rights"?).

The other problem homosexuals faced was the law itself. In most states sodomy is a crime. At this writing, roughly half the states consider even consensual sodomy between adults either a felony or a misdemeanor.[4]

Sodomy was forbidden by the laws of all the 13 original states at the time the Bill of Rights was ratified.[5] A group can hardly achieve total social acceptance when society has already decided to make what they do criminal and punishable by imprisonment.

## Q

How did homosexuals attempt to overcome the negative language used to describe them?

## A

The homosexuals chose a word unrelated to their behavior: "Gay" suggests what one is, not what one does. Those who promote "gay rights" must focus the legal and political discussion on the status of homosexuals as a minority and not on their behavior.

## Q

How are homosexuals trying to surmount the fact that the activity which defines their group is illegal in so many states?

## A

One approach to this legal problem is to use political or judicial means to invalidate these laws. In some states homosexuals have succeeded.

But they have learned that a more sensible strategy is to avoid that legal thicket altogether. Using the emotional power of appeals for "rights" against "discrimination," homosexuals propose ordinances that forbid "discrimination" in housing, employment and public accommodations based on a person's "affectional or sexual preference" or "affectional or sexual orientation."[6]

# Q

**What is the purpose of the ordinances that homosexuals promote?**

# A

Proposed gay rights laws seek to protect homosexual groups' "rights." This demand for legislation assumes that homosexuals' rights have been abridged by social prejudice. Once that assumption is accepted, the homosexual appeal has the ring of common sense.

# Q

**While we may disagree with what homosexuals do, should we not at least acknowledge their rights, or at least not deny them rights shared by other Americans?**

# A

Homosexuals have legal rights identical to those of other citizens. Homosexuals are covered by all the protection of the Bill of Rights: they have a right to free speech, to petition the government, to bear arms, to assemble together peacefully, to choose any religion or none, to own property, to travel abroad, to buy and sell and to have due process of law in any criminal trial. They have access to the courts and to other legal constitutional protection of American citizenship.

# Q

**If new "rights" are created for homosexuals, are additional duties created for everyone else?**

# A

Yes. If their sexual behavior is given special protection in the form of "rights," that means rights will be taken away from others. If homosexuals have the right to teach sex education courses in the public schools, for example, the school must allow them to do so. The parent of a child in that school loses his or her say in determining the requisite moral qualifications of the teacher of that child.

# Q

**What is the difference between minorities now protected by civil rights laws and the homosexual minority?**

# A

Saying homosexual behavior deserves the specially protected status of racial and religious minorities makes no sense. It expands such laws from their initial limits—protecting a particular unchangeable and morally neutral status like race—to include, at least potentially, an entire galaxy of perverted behavior.

Civil rights laws have always required a careful balancing of social interests. On the one hand society benefits from such historic freedoms as that of association. On the other hand, society also benefits when arbitrary decisions that cause substantial injury to innocent parties are discouraged. Civil rights laws strike a delicate balance between these interests. Such laws give substantial relief to victims of prejudice by forbidding arbitrary or irrational decisions generally without limiting the right of anyone to make decisions based on reasonable criteria.

# Q

**Is there any objective, concrete way to define groups that *do* merit the protection of civil rights laws?**

# A

Human rights laws typically protect classes of people defined by extraordinary circumstances. Such groups have historically met these five requirements:

(1) *A demonstrable pattern of discrimination.* Law will only intervene when a demonstrable and pervasive practice of discrimination exists throughout society.

(2) *Causing substantial injury.* The civil rights movement, focusing particularly on racial minorities, introduced volumes of reports showing substantial economic injury to minorities caused by discrimination.

(3) *To a class of people with an unchangeable status.* Because those protected by civil rights laws are bound together by status, not preference or moral character or forms of behavior, they can argue that they cannot change their indelible characteristic to accommodate society. Race, color and sex are fixed genetically. National origin is fixed historically. Although religious affiliations change, religion is generally not considered a "whimsical preference." Religion, to the true believer, is as unchangeable as race. Except for gay rights laws, no human rights law protects behavior. Certainly *none protects preferences.*

(4) *No element of moral*

*fault.* The classes normally protected by civil rights laws are morally neutral. No moral fault is attached to being black, a native or an immigrant, a male or a female. On the other hand, social stigma attends those who flaunt immoral lifestyles. For example, the inveterate liar suffers social isolation, and customers stop shopping at a business owned by a cheat. Present civil rights laws focus on groups that all agree are morally neutral.

**(5)** ***Based on criteria that are not arbitrary and irrational.*** Civil rights laws do not limit the right of people to make rational choices. They simply cancel a license to be prejudiced or to indulge irrational whims. For example, a person's skin color tells nothing

# Do homosexuals have a constitutional right to commit sodomy?

Although gay rights movement activists have concentrated on promoting gay rights ordinances, they have not abandoned their attack on existing criminal sodomy statutes. As long as their behavior remains criminal, it is hard for them to argue that they deserve special social protection for it. When challenging sodomy statutes, homosexuals argue that there is a "right to privacy" in the penumbras of the Constitution which protects private acts of consensual sodomy.

In making that argument, homosexuals rely on cases that interpret the Constitution as forbidding government interference with private decisions. And so for example, a consensual "right of privacy" has been held to protect decisions about education and child-rearing choices,[11] marriage[12] and, more recently, contraception[13] and abortion.[14]

Homosexuals have argued from these cases that just as the law cannot unconditionally forbid a couple from using birth control (the *Griswold* case), it cannot forbid two consenting adults from committing sodomy in the privacy of a bedroom.

Although homosexuals had some initial success in state and federal courts using such arguments,[15] the Supreme Court settled the question in *Bowers v. Hardwick*.[16] Mr. Hardwick had brought suit in Federal District Court, challenging the constitutionality of the Georgia sodomy statute insofar as it criminalized consensual sodomy. He lost at the district court level, but won on appeal to the Court of Appeals, which held that the Georgia statute violated his fundamental rights.

The Supreme Court disagreed.

about his or her capacity to be a successful employee. Whether an individual is Presbyterian or Methodist does not tell whether he or she might make a good tenant. Taking away the right to make irrational decisions, therefore, takes away nothing significant.

# Q
**Don't homosexuals deserve special protection because they are so often discriminated against?**

# A
Homosexuals can show neither a demonstrable pattern of discrimination nor substantial injury. Indeed, homosexuals control substantial wealth, are often style setters in major communities and have undeni-

---

In a vigorously written opinion, Justice White wrote:

Precedent aside, however, Respondent would have us announce, as the Court of Appeals did, a fundamental right to engage in homosexual sodomy. This we are quite unwilling to do.[17]

Justice White pointed out that any fundamental liberties protected by a right to privacy must be "implicit in the concept of ordered liberty," or deeply rooted "in the nation's history and tradition."[18] Because sodomy was traditionally a criminal offense in all states, he suggested, to find that a right to engage in anal or oral sodomy was deeply rooted in this nation's history and tradition or is "implicit in the concept of ordered liberty" would be "at best facetious."[19]

Summing up, the Court said: And if Respondent's submission is limited to the voluntary sexual conduct between consenting adults, it would be difficult, except by fiat, to limit the claimed right to homosexual conduct while leaving exposed to prosecution adultery, incest, and other sexual crimes, even though they are committed in the home. We are unwilling to start down that road.[20]

In a concurring opinion, Justice Burger pointed out the moral dimension:

To hold that the act of homosexual sodomy is somehow protected as a fundamental right would be to cast aside millenia of moral teaching.[21]

Justice Burger's opinion paralleled a recent circuit court decision from the District of Columbia Court of Appeals which had approved the discharge of a homosexual from the military. Finding homosexuality "a form of behavior never before protected and indeed traditionally condemned. . . .,"[22] that Court held that its decision should be based on constitutional principle, not shifting public opinion.

able political power. As the *Washington Post* has pointed out, homosexuals have become a new "power bloc" that has both "power and money."[7]" As one homosexual author writes, the "dominant style of New York . . . is now set by gays."[8]

# Q

**But shouldn't homosexuals' rights be guaranteed because they can't help doing what they do?**

# A

The homosexual state is neither genetically fixed nor unchangeable. The most prominent psychiatric expert on homosexuality, Dr. Charles Socarides, a professor at the Albert Einstein College of Medicine, writes in the *Journal of Psychiatry*:

Homosexuality, the choice of a partner of the same sex for orgastic satisfaction, is not innate. There is no connection between sexual instinct and the choice of sexual object. Such an object choice is learned, acquired behavior: there is no inevitable genetically inborn propensity towards the choice of a partner of either the same or op-posite sex.[9]

Dr. Socarides goes on to say that "psychotherapy appears to be unsuccessful [in changing homosexual behavior] in only a small number of patients of any age in whom a long habit is combined with . . . lack of desire to change."[10]

# Q

**Is homosexuality a moral issue or a morally neutral one like race or sex that merits the protection of civil rights laws?**

# A

For most people, homosexuality remains a moral issue and moral fault is attached to homosexual behavior. This belief is deeply rooted, beginning with primitive taboos and the teachings of both the Old and the New Testaments (see chapters two and three in this book).

# Q

**But isn't it irrational to consider a person's sexual orientation when dealing with them in everyday life?**

# A

Taking into account a person's homosexuality is by no means irrational in many circumstances. Suppose, for example, a supervisor must hire an employee for a day-care center. Who will be a better employee—a person whose skin is pigmented black, brown, white, yellow or red? Should the supervisor choose a Methodist over a Presbyterian? Is a Swiss a better diaper changer than an Austrian? If one answers such silly questions at all, the only reasonable response must be, "It depends"—depends, of course, on the character of the individual. Whether the applicant is black, Presbyterian or Swiss is of no interest to the rational decision-maker.

But taking into account a person's perverted sexual orientation is neither arbitrary nor irrational in such a case. The supervisor may know that the applicant, an average homosexual, is statistically a significant health risk, being peculiarly susceptible to infections that are especially dangerous for young children. The supervisor may also believe the person's promiscuity makes him an inappropriate role model for children. Is it socially responsible to make it illegal for this supervisor to consider such relevant factors? Is the law prepared to force us to ignore facts that our common sense, moral convictions and increasing medical knowledge tell us are relevant?

# Q

**Is there any truth to the argument that gay rights laws open the door to more radical legislation?**

# A

Yes. Gay rights laws are not the ultimate objective. They are simply a way station en route to what homosexuals really want: full social acceptance.

The 1972 gay rights platform shows the breadth of these objectives.[23] It contains, among others, the following demands:

Issuance by the President of an executive order prohibiting discrimination in the federal civil service because of sexual orientation in hiring and promoting; and prohibiting discrimination against homosexuals in security clearances.

Elimination of tax inequities victimizing single persons and same-sex couples.

Federal encouragement and support for sex education courses, prepared and taught by gay women and men, presenting homosexuality as a valid, healthy preference and lifestyle as a viable alternative to heterosexuality.

Federal funding of aid programs of gay men's and women's organizations designed to alleviate the problems encountered by gay women and men which are engendered by an oppressive sexist society.

Repeal of all laws prohibiting transvestism and cross dressing.

Repeal of all laws governing the age of sexual consent.

Repeal of all legislative provisions that restrict the sex or number of per-

---

## Civil Rights Denied in Big Brothers Case

While many extol the liberating effects of gay rights laws, few focus on their coercive impact. Most of these laws carry criminal penalties. The Big Brothers case in Minneapolis is an example of this problem. In 1977 a young man in Minneapolis applied to be a volunteer for the "Big Brothers" organization. Big Brothers attempts to introduce fatherless boys to men who can serve as male role models. Because of the increasing number of single parent families, Big Brothers organizations throughout the country face growing numbers of requests from mothers who want Big Brothers to take their sons fishing, camping, hiking and to other recreational activities the mother may feel herself unable to provide.

While reviewing the applicant's resume during the interview, the Big Brothers' representative noticed several items that suggested homosexual affiliations. He asked the applicant whether he was a homosexual. The man admitted he was. Despite this revelation, the interview was not terminated. The interviewer mentioned that Big Brothers has a policy of revealing all known facts about potential Big Brothers to the mothers of their clients, who have the last word on the suitability of any applicant. If any of the facts are worrisome to the mother, she can decide to reject the man as a Big Brother for her son. If none of the facts is objectionable, she can accept the proposed Big Brother. The interviewer explained to the applicant that if the mother had no objections to his homosexuality, he would be a Big Brother. It was her right to decide.

But t even this liberal, apparently liberal policy did not satisfy the man who wanted to be a Big Brother. He immediately

sons entering into a marriage unit; and the extension of legal benefits to all persons who cohabit regardless of sex or numbers.

## Q

**What sort of influence do gay activists hope to have in our nation's schools?**

## A

Homosexual activists like Jean O'Leary, a prominent lesbian once appointed by Jimmy Carter to the National Commission for the Observance of International Women's Year, suggest a radical agenda. In a paper called "Lesbians and the Schools," O'Leary demands that schools offer sex education

sued under the Minneapolis gay rights ordinance, alleging that he had been discriminated against as a homosexual. The mere fact that his homosexuality would be made known to the mother, he argued, would likely lead to his disqualification as a Big Brother. He was thus being discriminated against for his affectional preference.

Big Brothers argued that this policy is not discriminatory. It makes no comments, negative or positive, about potential Big Brothers. Its representatives simply reveal all the facts, including other protected classes in the human rights law—race, color, age, religion, sex, marital status and the like. The decision is left up to the mother.

Despite this fair-sounding rationale, the Human Rights Hearing Officer in Minneapolis found Big Brothers guilty of discrimination under the ordinance. He imposed costs on the organization of more than $6,000 and re-

quired Big Brothers to accept homosexuals without disclosing their homosexual preference to mothers of sons who might go on weekend outings with them. In addition, the officer required "affirmative action." Big Brothers was told to advertise in two newspapers in the San Francisco area read exclusively by homosexuals. Although the Human Rights Hearing Officer's decision was later reversed by a district court judge, Big Brothers incurred enormous expenses. Rather than risk such financial disaster again, Big Brothers gave in. In the fall of 1983 they announced a "national policy of accepting 'gay' men as prospective brothers to fatherless youth, 6-16 years old, unless the man is 'unstable' or has a 'poor lifestyle.'"

This is only one example of several similar problems caused by gay rights ordinances.[24]

courses "to encourage students to explore alternative lifestyles, including lesbianism," that school libraries include books extolling homosexuals, that homosexual clubs be established in schools to "foster a community of spirit" among homosexuals and that books that disparage homosexuality be banned. She also recommends that students be given names of homosexual counseling services available in the community and that teachers of human sexuality courses take a "positive view" of homosexuality.

# Q

**Do homosexuals want their unions to have the same legal status as traditional marriages?**

# A

Yes. Many argue that homosexual partnerships merit the same benefits accorded heterosexual marriage. By explicit social policy, married couples can file joint tax returns, inherit property, use gift and estate tax mechanisms to maximize their estate, bring wrongful death actions on behalf of a spouse and enjoy a host of other legal benefits. Homosexuals want the same advantages for their frequent-

ly transitory relationships.

Several jurisdictions are considering domestic partnership legislation. The Berkeley City Council passed such a policy in January, 1985. The San Francisco City Council passed the ordinance but it was vetoed by Mayor Dianne Feinstein. Similar legislation is under consideration elsewhere.

Gay rights laws can be used as a foot in the door to such social experimentation. If discrimination against homosexuals is wrong, shouldn't their "marriages" enjoy all legal privileges?

# Q

**What do proposals to make illegal the "demeaning" of a sexual orientation mean?**

# A

Several gay rights laws include provisions making it unlawful to "deride" or "denigrate" homosexual status. While these laws aim to discourage the taunting of homosexuals, their application could include criminal penalties for ministers who express from the pulpit the view that homosexuals' acts are immoral.

Some argue that such laws

merely proscribe "terroristic threats." But, if this were true, these proposals would add nothing to laws already in existence that declare threats or assaultive language illegal regardless of the sexual orientation of the victim. And some of these laws go further. An ordinance proposed to the Seattle City Council would have made it illegal to "discredit, demoralize, or belittle another person by words or conduct" based on sexual orientation. A Seattle prosecutor commented it would be a "new tool" in his arsenal. This tool is unfortunately so blunt that it could be used against those who "belittle" or "discredit" homosexuals by calling sodomy perverted or sinful.

# Q

**Do gay rights laws cause people to violate their consciences?**

# A

As Justice White notes in his decision in *Bowers v. Hardwick,* homosexual behavior has traditionally been condemned and is morally repugnant to many people of varying religious persuasions. Such laws might compel religious schools or other religious organiza-

tions to hire persons whose sexual practices contradict their religious beliefs. These laws could force religious organizations that operate battered women's shelters or children's day-care centers to hire homosexuals or risk losing government funding.

Those who sincerely wish to make judgments based on perceived moral character face a hopeless predicament: violate the conscience or violate the law. This is, of course, inconsistent with the purpose of civil rights laws as expressed by Dr. Martin Luther King, who dreamed of a day when his children would be judged by the "content of their character" rather than by the "color of their skin."

# Q

**Does society have a right to prefer heterosexual behavior as a matter of social policy?**

# A

Society needs not be ashamed of promoting the family. Strong families are the foundation of a strong society. Families are microcosms of society, providing essential services like procreation, education, welfare and training. It is more than a particular form of sexual expression.

As Justice Harlan once wrote:

> The right of privacy most manifestly is not an absolute. Thus, I would not suggest that adultery, homosexuality, fornication and incest are immune from criminal enquiry, however privately practiced . . . but the intimacy of husband and wife is necessarily an essential and accepted feature of the institution of marriage, an institution which the State not only must allow but which always and in every age it has fostered and protected.[25]

Homosexuality, on the other hand, is essentially anti-family in its acceptance of promiscuous sexuality and socially irresponsible behavior.[26]

# Q

**Why should social acceptance be withheld from so-called immoral behavior?**

# A

Conventional wisdom tells us that to tolerate weakness is often a virtue; to encourage immorality is always a vice. Gay rights laws that give special protection and privileges to people who practice sexual perversion reward immorality.

For example, anyone who has dealt with men who expose themselves knows the terrible shame they experience. Wrestling with a strange compulsion they find almost impossible to control, they expose themselves in public libraries or on street corners. They appear in court—often dressed in jail-supplied paper suits—too ashamed to talk about their activity to court-appointed lawyers. It is one thing to feel compassion for them. It is quite another to join with them in a parade down Fifth Avenue dressed in raincoats and carrying placards celebrating "Flashers' Pride."

Similar examples abound. Recovering alcoholics deserve our applause, but a city council approving "Drunkards' Pride Day," replete with public intoxication, would be a monstrosity. Everyone admires the Augustine who repents from his hedonistic lifestyle and lives a life of Christian purity. But a publicly celebrated "Adulterers' Pride Day" should be viewed with contempt.

Public officials nonetheless

often rush to be identified with "Gay Pride." No one should take pride in immoral behavior, or, even worse, encourage others to take pride in behavior that is destroying them.

# Q

**Why do some people say sodomy is the most dangerous activity in America and should not, therefore, be given special protection?**

# A

The medical consequences of homosexuality are alarming. AIDS, probably transmitted most efficiently by anal sodomy, threatens to destroy entire nations and may become the most gruesome epidemic in history (for more information on AIDS, see chapter one).

But the medical community knew the health risks associated with homosexuality long before the emergence of AIDS. Medical specialists knew the disproportionate impact on the homosexual community of diseases like gonorrhea, syphilis, hepatitis A, hepatitis, cytomegalovirus, amoebic bowel disease ("gay bowel syndrome") and herpes. Although homosexuals may be only five percent (some estimate 10 percent) of the U.S. population, they carry over 44 percent of the nation's cases of syphilis, 51 percent of gonorrhea of the throat and 53 percent of intestinal infections. Forty percent of homosexuals have gonorrhea infections. Diseased homosexual food handlers in public restaurants have been responsible for major outbreaks of amebiasis and hepatitis A infections in San Francisco and Minneapolis; homosexuals have a rate of infectious hepatitis B some 20 to 50 times greater than heterosexual males. It is no wonder that Dr. Selma Dritz, an official of the San Francisco Department of Public Health, wrote that "special precautions are required to protect the public from carriers who work as food handlers, bartenders, attendants in medical care facilities and as teachers and aids in day-care centers for infants and young children."

While gay rights laws have been in effect for the last decade in San Francisco, the city has seen its venereal disease rate rise to 22 times the national average; infectious hepatitis A increased 100 percent, infectious hepatitis B 300 percent; amoebic colon infections increased 2,500 percent. Venereal disease clinics in the city saw 75,000 patients every year, of whom close to 80 percent were homosexual males; 20 percent of them carried rectal gonorrhea. *New York Times Magazine* quotes a doctor familiar with the homosexual populace as saying that the "average homosexual" is a "tropical island of exotic diseases." That this is no overstatement is confirmed by a survey conducted by the American Public Health Association, using questionnaires sent to 1,800 organizations listed by the National Gay Task Force. Among other things, the survey revealed that 78 percent of homosexuals had had at least one sexually transmitted disease.

The gruesome prospects of AIDS need not be amplified here,[27] but it is known that sodomy is among the most efficient methods of transmitting the disease. To encourage such sexual practices at this time in history makes no sense.

## Q

**But aren't heterosexuals frequently equally perverted?**

## A

Homosexuals often point out the many examples of perverted sexual behavior among heterosexuals: child molesters, rapists, family incest, adulterers, whoremongers and other illicit sexual activity found among heterosexuals.

Such arguments, however, miss the point. No one is promoting special civil rights protection for these groups. They do not have any such protection at the present time and are often prosecuted. No greater rationale exists for creating new laws to protect "adulterers' rights" or "child molesters' rights" than exists for creating "gay rights."

## Q

**Isn't providing homosexuals with "gay rights" consistent with Christian compassion?**

## A

The homosexual, without doubt, deserves our compassion on a personal basis. But compassion is not shown by pretending that homosexual behavior is normal or healthy, any more than by pretending that an alcoholic should celebrate his alcoholism. To show compassion to homosexuals we must treat them as responsible moral beings who can change their behavior. Compassion must also be shown the innocent victims of homosexuals—those who are medically or psychologically damaged by them. To give homosexuals special treatment or to accept their lifestyle as healthy shows compassion neither to the homosexual nor to society at large.

# Q

**Shouldn't a person be able to do what he or she wants to in the privacy of his or her bedroom?**

# A

Although this argument makes a nice slogan, it does not withstand close analysis. If this principle were really the law, society could not protect itself from incest, child abuse, bigamy, prostitution, rape and a host of other private acts that have substantial social consequences. Society is, under proper circumstances, very concerned about what goes on in the privacy of the bedroom and quite frequently decides to make such conduct criminal.

# 5

# How to Minister to the Homosexual

## William H. McKain Jr.

As more and more homosexuals become public about their lifestyle, the church must learn how to extend ministry to the homosexual as a person without condoning the practice of homosexuality.

## Q

**Does the Christian have a ministry particularly to the homosexual?**

## A

Many insist that no spiritual mandate is given for a specific ministry to homosexual persons; the problems, principles and call to Christian ministry are the same regardless of sexual orientation. The position of this study is that *homosexual activity is contrary to God's re-vealed will and does indeed present unique needs to which the church must endeavor to minister.* Such ministry must not only relate to the homosexual person but also deal with the broader issues created by homosexuality and society's attitude toward it. The church must also endeavor to separate the AIDS crisis from the issues of homosexuality. The temptation for the church to use the AIDS epidemic to promote or condemn homosexuality can frustrate the church's efforts to deal with either issue.

**Bill McKain** is Director of the Department of Pastoral Care at Methodist Evangelical Hospital in Louisville, Kentucky. He holds degrees from the University of Illinois, B.S.; Asbury Theological Seminary, M.Div.; and Boston University School of Theology, Th.D. Dr. McKain was a consulting petroleum geologist for 11 years prior to receiving his theological education. He taught at Asbury Theological Seminary for five and one-half years. He is a Diplomate in the American Association of Pastoral Counselors, a Clinical member in the American Association for Marriage and Family Therapy and a supervisor in the Association for Clinical Pastoral Education.

# Q

**How do pro-homosexual advocates hope to influence today's churches?**

# A

Contrary to the traditional view of homosexuality, some within the church now contend that homosexuality is a "glorious gift of God." They say that the church should welcome homosexuals without restraints on or questions about their sexual lifestyle. Homosexuals should be ordained into the Christian ministry, some church leaders argue, and the church should sanction the so-called marriages of those homosexual persons whose relationship is claimed to be based on love, devotion and personal responsibility. Further, some now believe that the church should encourage young persons to choose their lifestyle, whether homosexual or heterosexual. Role models of both should be presented impartially.

# Q

**Is this pro-homosexual movement having any success?**

# A

Support for this position is gaining momentum. It is becoming more visible if not in fact winning the approval of more people. Homosexuals may constitute as much as 10 percent of the U.S. population—or 22 million men and women. Literally tons of literature are now available on the subject, including a *Journal of Homosexuality*. Yet the church is very much torn over the issues. Homosexual religious groups have emerged and have formed their own organizations in both Protestant and Roman Catholic circles. Well-known theologians and clergy openly avow their homosexual orientation and have published autobiographies of their experiences.[1] Many Protestant denominations agonize over the issues and the current contention that homosexuality is a normal lifestyle. Such pro-homosexual points of view are even coming from avowed "fundamentalist Christians."[2] What the church concludes about the issue has many and complex ramifications.

# Q

**Why hasn't the church been more successful in dealing with the issue of homosexuality?**

# A

Expecting the church to minister to homosexual persons and deal with the larger issues homosexuality presents is a great challenge. For generations the church has exhibited a largely repressive attitude toward sex in general. It thereby abdicated responsibility to lead society in an important and critical area of life. Further, the church's silence has also contributed to society's current obsession with sex; for suppression of a natural drive normally will lead to undue curiosity, exploitation and compulsiveness.

The church is beginning to accept responsibility to deal with human sexuality. But, as so often in its history, this comes only in response to a strong challenge from the secular world. Christian writers are now addressing the issues of human sexuality, but relatively few sermons are preached on the subject. Many, many believers remain guilt-ridden and fearful about their sexuality. In one survey of a church group, a young married woman said, "I know sex is okay in marriage, but somehow I just can't seem to rid myself of my upbringing which led me to believe it is wrong."

Therefore, it is asking much of the church to demand that it suddenly reverse its attitude and respond without fear or prejudice to the issues raised in this book. Lacking a clear understanding of one's own sexuality places great stress on a person (or an institution) if one is to respond with wisdom and compassion to homosexuality in the church.

# Q

**To what extent is the community of homosexual persons open to ministry from the church and what kind of ministry will it accept?**

# A

Barbara B. Gittings maintains that,

the majority of homosexuals would not change even if they could. More important, they should not change even if they could. What the homosexual wants—and here he or she is neither willing to compromise nor morally required to compromise— is acceptance of homosexuality as a way of life fully on par with heterosexuality, acceptance of the homosexual as a person on par with the heterosexual and acceptance of homosexuals as children of God on an equal basis with heterosexuals.[3]

She further maintains that ministry to the homosexual should be of the same type that is rendered as a matter of course to heterosexuals. Ministry should be supplied in a spirit of acceptance and "not in a spirit of missionary zeal to convert us to heterosexuality."[4] Many homosexuals believe that a change in their sexual orientation would violate their personhood and constitute a rejection of their spiritual calling. Homosexual religious groups such as the Metropolitan Community Church and its Roman Catholic counterpart, Dignity, believe they have a special ministry to the church. Their drawing apart into separate groups is only to enlighten the church. They are "working toward the day when it (MCC) can close its doors because the other Christian communities with love and understanding will have opened theirs to the gay people."[5]

These attitudes do not represent all homosexual persons. But it seems certain that there are many homosexuals who do not wish to convert to heterosexuality or receive the ministry of the church if that involves rejecting their homosexual practice. Typically our society today encourages the homosexual to accept his or her lifestyle. Consider such self-help books as *Positively Gay*[6] and works for therapists such as *Integrated Identity For Gay Men and Lesbians.*[7]

# Q

**What is a homosexual person?**

# A

We first must define what we mean by a "homosexual person." For our purposes we will not attempt a comprehensive definition that takes into account the many factors of causation, patterns of homosexual practice and the personality of the homosexual. It is enough to say that a homosexual person is an individual who is motivated in his or her adult life by a definite preferential erotic attraction to members of the same sex and who usually, but not always, engages in overt sexual relations with persons of the same sex. Reference to adults in this definition excludes the occasional adolescent experimentation the pastor may encounter in his/her youth group. Definite preference for the same sex excludes persons in situations such as prisons where there is little or no opportunity for heterosexual expression. Also, this working definition indicates that a homosexual person may or may not engage in overt homosexual relations.

# Q

**What is mental health, and how can we know whether gays—or other people—have achieved it?**

# A

Even when we use our own rulers, mental health is an elusive object, and opinions vary as to what it is. Paul Tournier made this point when speaking on mental health at McCormick Seminary in Chicago. He quotes Claude Weil, former secretary of the General Congress of the World Health Organization for Mental Health, who said that the definition of mental health has been much discussed and debated but has never been resolved in a satisfactory manner. Weil says that as a general rule it is easier to define negative concepts than positive ones. Thus, adds Tournier, "the most important treatises on medicine start with

the subject of pathology, and during the whole of his life a doctor is constantly endeavoring to bring man to normality, without ever knowing precisely what a normal man is."[8]

Tournier observes that Freud's goals in psychoanalysis were to "give a man the capacity to enjoy and to work."[9] Tournier contends that we must add to these some criteria of human plenitude, fulfillment and flowering.

Tournier said also that Henri Duchesne, one of the founders of the International League of Mental Health, has three criteria for mental health: adaptation to one's milieu, acceptance of sexuality and aptitude and talent for happiness. The two latter, he observes, are similar to Freud's criteria. The criterion of adaptation to one's milieu is the one that Tournier believes is problematical. It is the most critical criterion in considering the reports of Bell, Hooker and others that lead to conclusions that adaptation and adjustment are synonymous with the good life.

# Q

**But if homosexuals are sometimes "well adjusted," what's the problem?**

# A

Many view adaptation and adjustment as a criterion for mental health. But they fail to recognize that adaptation to one's milieu is adaptation to a disordered state because of our fallen nature and our existence in a disordered world. As the apostle Paul indicates in Romans 8, both the children of God and creation are groaning to be delivered from bondage. "Neurosis," says Tournier, "is an effort to adapt oneself to a world that is unbalanced and out of order. . . .Illness appears frequently as an attempt to find a cure."[10] It does not provide satisfaction, however, because it is precisely an attempt to provide adaptation to a disordered milieu. The treatment of symptoms of neurosis—and of homosexuality—without attention to spiritual health and God's plan for humankind is dangerous. It is dangerous because the struggle and movement involved in the illness is an expression of the struggle of the spirit in a disordered world.

# Q

**Do all the experts agree that homosexuals are as well adjusted as everyone else?**

# A

No. Not all authorities from the behavioral sciences believe that homosexual practice is compatible with the good life. Bieber, Bergler, Socarides, Kronemeyer and others, apart from any theological consideration, contend that homosexuality is a deviant from the normal and represents a maladaptation of the personality. The reports from empirical studies are by no means unanimously pro-homosexual.

# Q

**How then does homosexuality relate to the "good life?**

# A

Tournier's insistence on responsibility toward God as a key factor in experiencing the good life is important in understanding the good life as it relates to sexuality. Responsibility implies expectations on the part of the one toward whom one is to be responsible. The task each of us must face then is asking what the Creator expects of us concerning our sexuality. Only in responsibly meeting those expectations can we experience the good life. Any variance is less than good, or worse, depending on the issue.

# Q

**What is God's will concerning sex?**

# A

The biblical view of homosexuality is very ably explored in other chapters of this book. Two points need to be reiterated here, however. First, the Bible makes it clear, and on this most Christians will agree, that sexuality is a gift of God. Its purposes are at least threefold: (1) procreation; (2) to be an expression of love and one-fleshness; and (3) to symbolize the most holy relationship known to humankind, the relationship between Christ and His church.

God has revealed His will concerning certain boundaries within which we may express our sexuality. Those boundaries confine sexual expression to heterosexual marriage—not before marriage, not outside of marriage, but in marriage between two people of the opposite sex. Everywhere homosexuality is discussed in the Bible it is forbidden, while the Scriptures everywhere affirm heterosexual love in marriage as the context in which God expects us to express our sexuality. True,

Jesus did not speak to the issue of homosexuality. However, if it is a viable lifestyle, one wonders why He didn't affirm it. He did affirm God's will for heterosexual marriage and the goal of one-fleshness. As Bennett J. Sims has written in a very fine article, sexuality "is not humanity's gift to itself; it is God's bestowal and it carries conditions."[11] The Giver of this gift has declared the bounds within which we shall use it. To exercise this gift in a homosexual context is clearly outside the bounds of God's revealed will.

# Q

**Why is the concept of "one-flesh" (i.e., heterosexual marriage) so important?**

# A

The mystical symbolism of marriage as a representation of the relationship between Christ and His church involves both the concept of one-fleshness and the fact that we are created in the image of God. Therefore, Sims states,

> In regard to the image of God it is crucial to any Christian understanding of sex that the divine image in humanity is incomplete without both

man and woman. Which is to hold that the aim of Christian sexuality is not personal satisfaction but interpersonal completeness. "The two shall become one flesh" (see Gen. 2:24 and Mark 10:8). This is the ancient prescription. One plus one equals one: completeness. It remains a great mystery since human experience is imperfect, even in rapture. But from the mystery we can discern the meaning of the ideal of completeness, which is the *union of opposites*, or the coming together of differences (though this is fundamental to a biblical understanding of sexuality), but such differences as personality, temperament, social function and aspiration, all gathered in a physical symbol of genital differentiation.[12]

The natural conclusion to this position is that homosexuality is a distortion of the divine intent and therefore contrary to any conception of the good life and sexuality.

Q

**But isn't this biblical view of sexuality difficult for heter-** osexuals as well as homosexuals?

A

Exactly. Whether one's orientation is homosexual or heterosexual, continual tensions are inherent in being steward over one's sexuality. For the single, the married and the have-been-married, the guidelines are the same. Therefore, if one's lot in life does not afford opportunity for sexual expression within God's prescribed boundaries (heterosexual marriage), then the door to sexual expression with another human being is closed regardless of the sex of the partner chosen. Even in the context of heterosexual marriage, the need for stewardship in the expression of sexuality is not waived. All of the principles of loving one's neighbors and relating to them in the way that best fulfills them personally apply. And one's mate is, after all, one's closest neighbor. There is no room in marriage for lust, manipulation of the other person, selfishness, power struggles, control and so forth. Therefore,

homosexuals are not beings apart in humanity. They have no sex problem essentially different from

# Statistics on Homosexuality

The Bell research discussed previously also revealed that of the 979 homosexual persons with whom they had two- to five-hour interviews, 25 percent believed that homosexuality was an emotional disorder and about one-third had seriously considered stopping all homosexual activity at some point in their lives. Further, "The average male (homosexual person) reported sex acts with hundreds of men, and two-thirds had developed venereal disease at least once. Forty percent of the men had had more than 500 sex partners, and a quarter of them, as adults, had performed with boys under 16."[14]

These statistics vary between whites and blacks, and the Bell study indicated that 50 percent of the white homosexual males had had more than 500 different sexual partners.[15] In another place Bell made the following comment about their research:

A modal view of the white male homosexual, based on our findings, would be that of a person reporting 1,000 or more sexual partners throughout his lifetime, most of whom were strangers prior to their sexual meeting and with whom sexual activity occurred only once. Only a few of these partners were persons for whom there was much care or affection or were ever seen socially again. During the past year, twenty-eight per-

cent reported having had more than fifty partners; however, thirty-one percent claimed to have ten partners or less.[16]

Dr. Walter H. Smartt, head of the department of venereal diseases in Los Angeles County, has reported that 50 percent of the syphilis and 20 percent of the gonorrhea in Los Angeles County is accounted for by homosexual persons.[17]

As of October 19, 1987, according to the statistics of the United States Centers for Disease Control, 66% of the diagnosed AIDS cases are among homosexual / bisexual males with another 8% of the cases being in a dual transmission category—those who are both homosexual male and IV drug abusers.

A 1978 news item noted: "An English group, the Paedophile Information Exchange, consisting almost exclusively of male homosexuals, is calling for the legal and social acceptance of paedophilia (sex with children), the recognition of what it calls "the need in Britain for a group of men and women sexually attracted to young people" and the lowering of the age of consent."[18]

Admittedly, statistics related to homosexuality, promiscuity, venereal disease, seduction of children and so forth are subject to various interpretations. The point is, however, that the headliners who write that "gay is good" don't mention all of the statistics.

that of other people, from that of the unmarried, the widowed or the married. For all, it is the same problem, namely, that of absolute obedience to God's will, in sex as in all other domains of life. A man who by a look "commits adultery in his heart," to use Christ's words, or a man who uses his wife otherwise than as God wills, is as disobedient, as sinful, as a homosexual who gives free play to his abnormal impulses. It can be quite as difficult for a married heterosexual really to obey God's will for his sexual life and to be absolutely pure in marriage as it is for a bachelor or a homosexual to observe an absolute sexual discipline.[13]

**Q**

**But if our sexuality is a gift from God, how can it be destructive, no matter what the context?**

**A**

Our sexuality is a God-given gift, like a fire in the home. In the fireplace the fire warms and fills the atmosphere with tranquillity by its flickering light and pleasant crackling. In the attic, however, it becomes a roaring rage that ravishes and eventually destroys the home it was intended to comfort. When we use our sexuality outside of the clear, God-given conditions stated in the Scriptures, our experience of the good life is thwarted, whether we recognize it at the moment or not. When women exchange natural relations for unnatural and men are consumed with passion for one another, they will receive "in themselves the due penalty for their perversion" (Rom. 1:27). Likewise, the person who commits fornication or adultery.

**Q**

**But if the church is to truly love the homosexual person, shouldn't it accept his or her homosexual behavior?**

**A**

Those who hold that homosexual practice is compatible with the good life appeal to the character of love. The church is asked to reverse its condemnation of homosexual practice and endorse it because homosexuality can be an appropriate expression of Christian love. Also, the appeal to love is used in an effort to instill guilt in those who disagree. As Muehl has so aptly stated, when anyone refuses to endorse the demands of the homosexual militants today and "presumes to suggest that this proposal requires careful examination and the review of a number of substantive theological issues, he or she is very likely to be accused of loveless bigotry and charged with causing great pain to some very sensitive people."[19] The appeal is that truly loving a homosexual person requires accepting homosexual practice. The fallacy in that appeal is obvious.

Love constrains us to relate to others according to their needs. However, that prescription sometimes requires me to relate to my children, my wife or my friends in ways that they do not prefer because love may not lead me to see their needs in the same way they do. Sometimes the need is to comfort my friend. Sometimes the need is for me to leave him in his solitude. Sometimes the need is for me to resurrect a conflict that stands in the way of our relationship and thus stay by his side when he would prefer me to leave. Loving behavior obviously cannot al-

ways be determined by the desires of the loved object. But, as Muehl also writes, "'God is love'—so runs the argument. Anything that is an expression of love is good. Since same-gender sex is an expression of love, it should be blessed by the church."[20] He tags this as a "classic example of questions-begging" and then states further, "One of the most popular errors in the realm of Christian ethics has been the effort to make love an omnipotent spiritual quality which has the power to sanctify anything that is done in its name."[21]

# Q

**But can't true love make a homosexual relationship good in God's eyes?**

# A

No. Love does not give us license to transcend the requirements of responsibility in our relationships but rather requires us to express ourselves in appropriate and certain ways. Indeed, Muehl summarizes,

> Love establishes the modes of interpersonal relating. It does not simply consecrate those that we find pleasant or profitable.

Thus, love does not always justify sexual union. It frequently makes it clear that sexual union is grossly inappropriate to a relationship. It is wrong for fathers to act out their love for their daughters in coition, for mothers to take their sons to bed, for brothers and sisters to copulate. Only the sickest minds would hold otherwise. And once we have established that fact the argument that homosexual union is good simply because it is motivated by love falls of its own weight. It is every bit as likely that the love of man for man or woman for woman bids them refrain from sexual intercourse as that it urges them into it.

For the purpose of making such statements about the argument that same-gender sex is an expression however inappropriate, of love, I have assumed that some form of affection is, indeed, the driving force in gay relationships. This is by no means incontrovertibly established. A number of authorities in the field argue that the dynamic of homosexuality is not love for the same sex but hatred or fear of the opposite sex. Men who take other men to bed, they suggest, may be less interested in expressing affection for their partners than in displaying contempt for women. And the same would be true, *mutatis mutandis*, for lesbians.[22]

It becomes obvious that there is a clear relationship between true love, responsibility and the good life that the Creator has revealed to us. It also is obvious that any views on the good life will inevitably involve certain *a priori* faith assumptions.

# Q

**If homosexuality is so far removed from God's plan, why should the church care about homosexuals at all?**

# A

Doing what comes naturally is not necessarily the pathway to the good life, whether one is talking of sexuality or any other dimension of life. Rather it is responsibility that is the key factor. This applies to a consideration of ministry as well. If one views homosexuality according to the position expressed in this book, the natural tendency may be to condemn homosexual practice as well as persons who have a homosexual orientation and declare that we should come out from among them and be separate. That is, we should have nothing to do with the problem beyond rejecting homosexuality as contrary to that which leads to the good life.

The responsible thing to do, however, is to see the current problems that the church faces because of homosexuality as an opportunity for God to do something significant among us. This contradicts our tendency to be pessimistic because of the intensity of some of the problems involved in the issue. Because homosexual practice is seen by many in the church as a loathsome perversion in the midst of an already taboo area and because of the pessimistic prognosis for change heard from many quarters, it would be easy to despair and do nothing.

## Q
**If the church is to neither exclude homosexuals nor condone homosexual acts, what is the proper course?**

## A
Writing out of the context of his struggle as an avowed but non-practicing homosexual, Alex Davidson gives us a clue to the answer to this question:

I believe it's common for homosexuals to be obsessed with their sexual predicament to the point where they can think of nothing else, and I see the tendency in myself. There are more important matters in life than indulging in a good moan because one is made differently from one's neighbor. The neighbor may be envied for his blessedly uncomplicated heterosexual life, but he assuredly has some other burden he might justifiably moan about.[23]

The church likewise needs to develop a proper perspective on the problem. It should not throw up its hands in despair or hide its hands for fear of soiling them. The Christian gospel declares that God always does His greatest work in the most difficult situations. Davidson says in this regard, "When He [Christ] intends to make something wonderful He starts with a difficulty, and when He intends to make something very wonderful He starts with an impossibility."[24] The church should be optimistic and rejoice at the opportunity to minister to homosexual persons as a part of its ministry to the world. Out of the midst of a very difficult problem, God can do something significant. He can take our adversity and change it to advantage; He can work creatively in our conflicts.

## Q

**How should the church begin its ministry to homosexuals?**

## A

If the church is to be responsible in facing the problems of ministry to homosexual persons, its first task is to learn more about the problem of homosexuality. It is incumbent on anyone and any group proposing to minister in this area to learn about homosexuality. As a matter of fact, it is unfortunate that, in this scientific age when God's gift of knowledge is so liberally given, the church has not utilized more fully His gifts of technology and science for His purposes. But it is not too late.

## Q

**What are the causes of homosexuality?**

## A

Most writers who survey the data and opinions available on homosexuality conclude with one voice that the cause of homosexuality is a complex matter about which we really know very little of any conclusive nature. It is not within our scope here to consider in detail the causes of homosexuality. (See chapter six for an in-depth look at the causes of homosexuality.) A brief consideration of causes is in order, however, so that we may develop perspective on appropriate ministry.

Causes that have been posited can be arranged into three general groupings: (1) those related to inborn, or constitutional, factors; (2) parent-child and other family dynamics; and (3) external environmental influences.

## Q

**To what extent is the homosexual person responsible for his or her orientation?**

## A

Many homosexual persons contend that their sexual orientation is inborn and thus natural. Others studying the causes of homosexuality have conjectured that the orientation results from hormonal imbalances. In either instance, the appeal is to a natural genetic or physiological cause. Although these theories were popular among investigators earlier in the century, most experts now see little evidence that homosexuality is caused by either genetic factors or hormonal imbalances. Hooker states, for example:

People are not born homosexual, but there may be a genetic predisposition. Or it may take an indirect route; physique is influenced by heredity, and boys who have frail physiques may be more likely to become gay.

There is no evidence that homosexuals have faulty hormone levels, or that their sexual orientation can be changed with hormone injections. Hormone shots may increase the level of sexual desire, but they won't change where the desire is directed.[25]

Even if there were evidence to substantiate the position that some homosexuality is caused by genetic or hormonal factors, that would not necessarily dictate that homosexuality is a natural state. It could just as easily be interpreted theologically as an evidence of the Fall if it is believed that the fall of humankind is pervasive, and it seems obvious that it is, in the light of other congenital disorders that are unquestionably pathological.

# Q
## Does homosexuality begin early in life?

# A

Many writers agree on the theory that the sexual identity of the child is formed at a very early age, perhaps as early as two years. The factors involved are considered integral to the process. In the case of a developing homosexual person, the most critical of these factors is generally assumed to be an abnormal relationship with one or both of the parents—a relationship that results in a distorted or arrested psychosexual development. Various interpretations of the interactions of the dynamics involved come from the views of Freud, Bieber, Bergler and others.

# Q
## What patterns contribute to homosexual development?

# A

Busby lists nine different patterns of relationships between parents that may contribute to a faulty psychosexual development: (1) absence of intimacy of the mother and father; (2) the absent father, either by death or by divorce, coupled with a mother who is too "present"; (3) the punitive father coupled with a masochistic mother; (4) a passive father with a domineering mother who also relates to the boy in an overly protective or overly permissive way; (5) an aloof father coupled with a mother who is too close and overly involved; (6) a vulgar father coupled with a prudish mother, giving the child an impression that masculine sexuality is reprehensible; (7) both parents absent from the child before he is 12; (8) the idealized mother coupled with a block in the child's identifying with the father, resulting in overidentification with the mother; and (9) the idealized father (or older brother), resulting in a kind of hostile-dependency relationship with the father.[26] The complexity of these interactions is obvious.

Bell wrote,

With regard to etiology, a preliminary view of our own data leads me to suppose that just as there is such a diversity of adult homosexuality, so there are multiple routes into this orientation, routes which may well account for differences in the way particular persons experience and express their homosexuality as well as the nature of their psychological makeup and social adjustment.[27]

# Q

**To what extent does the home environment influence a homosexual?**

# A

Some think too much has been made of the parents' role in causing homosexuality. Yet, no one seems to discount the potential influence of the home and the probability that it is critical. Bieber gives some comfort in his conclusion that it is practically impossible for homosexuality to result in a home where the child has at least one sound relationship with either parent.

The home also has secondary influence because it is there that we gain the first inclinations that condition our reactions to our environment.

Therefore, even though environmental factors outside of the home can be significant, our morals, coping patterns and so forth are behaviors mostly learned in the home. At least they are most capable of being influenced by the home.

## Q

**Outside of the home, what environmental factors encourage homosexuality?**

## A

The environmental factors thought to cause homosexual orientation vary. Seduction by an older sibling or an older adult at a formative period may be a factor. If a boy appears effeminate, his classmates may treat him in a way that inclines him toward a homosexual orientation. Children who lack confidence in their capacity to relate to the opposite sex may gravitate toward same-sex partners as a less threatening way to find intimacy. It is thought that in some instances parents' grim warnings about heterosexual practice and accompanying silence about homosexual experiences may lead a child to seek the latter as acceptable behavior. Others believe the current moral climate that tolerates pornography, glorifies illicit sexual activity and even seeks exotic sexual perversions may contribute to homosexual orientation and practice. Ruth Tiffany Barnhouse also comments, "In societies where women are highly valued, homosexuality in both sexes is far less frequent."[28]

## Q

**Do most homosexuals consciously choose their sexual orientation?**

## A

Although these foregoing factors may influence some individuals, there also may be some persons who have a homosexual orientation as a result of their own conscious choices. It would appear, however, that most homosexuals seem to have been passive recipients of their orientation and find themselves attracted to members of the same sex without the involvement of their own conscious processes. This point needs to be seen very clearly when considering a ministry to a homosexual person. It will engender compassion if the minister grasps the significance of the homosexual person as a passive recipient of an inclination involving pain, misery, frustration and self-condemnation, as this problem so often does.

A short time ago I spent some three hours talking to a male homosexual in San Francisco who said he hated and loathed himself when, as a teenager, he began to struggle with homosexual tendencies. He grew up in the church, in fact in a parsonage family. At age 15 he experienced a nervous breakdown because of the bondage in which he found himself. We need to realize the depth and complexity of the problem.

# Q

**Is there a difference between a homosexual tendency and acting on that tendency?**

# A

Yes. The distinction between homosexual orientation and homosexual practice is entirely appropriate, even though the Bible does not explicitly make such a distinction. It appears to me that any concept of divine grace compels us to recognize that a homosexual orientation that is passively received but not practiced is not in itself condemned by the Scriptures. For the reader who may have diffi-

culty understanding the person who "finds" himself/herself attracted to members of the same sex, the self-descriptive struggles of Alex Davidson[29] or some similar work by a Christian homosexual person may prove to be helpful reading.

# Q

**Why do many people have difficulty developing an accepting attitude toward homosexuals?**

# A

Ministry to homosexual persons compels us to examine our attitudes toward homosexuals. John Patton reminds us that the term *homosexual* is often an adjective, and if that adjective threatens us, we may not be able to respond in love to the person to whom it may apply. "Probably all of us," he writes, "have thus been overcome by adjectives and have failed to see the person who is looking to us for help."[30]

A negative reaction to the adjective *homosexual* indicates what some have termed "homophobia" or "heterosexism." Because of faulty understanding, aversion, projection or other factors related to our own self-perception and sexual adjustment, we are prone to reject the person because of the label. The fact of the matter is, the word *homosexual* applies to only one segment of the person. It in no way represents the whole person. All of us are much more than our sex drives and sexual preferences. Homophobia results in rejection of the homosexual person. This rejection may be conscious or unconscious and it does not really matter which. Rejection is sensed by the other person, and it frustrates the chances of ministering to that person.

# Q

**How do we develop an accepting attitude toward homosexual people so necessary for ministry?**

# A

Ministry requires the one presuming to minister to have the capacity to see the other person apart from his/her problems. It requires the capacity to see that person's inherent worth and potential as one who was made in the image of God and whose problems are no more or no less sinful than that which are common to all humankind. Such capacity requires a basic emotional health and clear resolution of one's own sexual "hang-ups." This is

a difficult task because reactions to sexual matters frequently spring from deep within. Noted at the beginning of this chapter was the difficulty of the church's response to homosexuality today in the light of its deep suppression of sex in general. Our homophobia may be deep seated also. It can relate to a natural aversion to that which God has forbidden. Also, some psychologists believe that the roots of homophobia are unconscious connections we make between homosexuality and barrenness and death. In other words, it is something that we sense is contrary to a fulfilling life for the individual and the race.

It is, at any rate, incumbent upon any who would presume to minister to homosexual persons that they work through their feelings and attitudes about homosexuality. This will be evidenced by a successful effort to separate the adjective *homosexual* from the person involved. God's love, which has been shed abroad in our hearts, demands that it be so.

# Q

**But if I accept a homosexual person, am I not also approving his or her behavior?**

**A**

No. Acceptance of the person does not mean adopting a morally approving stance toward homosexual behavior. In the first place, it is impossible for one to set aside his or her moral convictions in a pastoral relationship. Don Browning has made it clear that all therapy, and we might add all ministry, takes place within an unavoidable moral context.[31] This context, as well as the moral convictions of the minister, will be an inevitable part of the dynamics of the situation. Whether or not ethics, morals or theology are ever discussed in a context of ministry, the moral convictions of the minister will unavoidably be communicated.

**Q**

Is there one best approach to ministering to gay people?

**A**

No. We must guard against stereotyping homosexual persons. As the findings of the Institute for Sex Research at Indiana University indicate, homosexual persons are just as varied as heterosexual persons. Therefore, relating to every homosexual person requires an original approach.

Since all persons, including those with a homosexual orientation, are one-of-a-kind, ministry is always a unique process. Needs and motivations will vary. Consequently, pastoral care or ministry in other ways may not necessarily have anything to do directly with homosexuality.

**Q**

How does our theology affect our ministry to homosexuals?

**A**

One's theology of homosexuality will determine the boundaries and direction that ministry will take with a homosexual person. See for yourself what a difference theology makes by contrasting the position of this book with, for instance, that of Norman Pittenger, who writes:

the church has enough theological assurance to move forward in helping the homosexual in his or her kind of union to live as faithfully and in intention as permanently as the heterosexual. That ought to be the purpose of our Christian counseling and our Christian dealing with the homosexual— not to call him a greater sinner than others, which he is not, but to assist him to become a great lover. I am convinced that a sound theological approach will do a good deal to bring about this day of acceptance, welcome, and support.[32]

# Q

**What areas of the church's ministry, if any, are available to the practicing homosexual?**

# A

What the church can offer by way of ministry to the homosexual person is limited if that person chooses to continue in homosexual practice. Such a lifestyle is contradictory to traditional Christian doctrine and, therefore, incompatible with the standards expected of those who are members of the body of Christ. Baptism, membership in a local congregation, marriage, ordination and other ministries of the church that are opportunities for those who are recognized as followers of Christ cannot be made available to an openly avowed, practicing homosexual person.

However, the practicing homosexual should be made to feel welcome at all church programs, including worship services and other group activities that are open to the general public and do not have member-

## What mistakes are often made in counseling homosexuals?

Some pitfalls exist in working with a homosexual person who wishes to change his/her sexual preferences, however. One is the tendency to focus on sexual dynamics, forgetting that those dynamics are actually symptoms of arrested or distorted development. This maladjustment is, in all probability, related to deprivation of relationships or distortions of them and/or an inadequate sense of personal worth. Majoring then on the sex-object choice in counseling may be counter productive.[40] We agree with Harvey that "what the homosexual needs more than the achievement of satisfactory sexual relationships is an inner sense of personal dignity and worth and the feeling of fulfilling a purpose in life."[41]

ship in the local congregation as a prerequisite. The following statement in the *Discipline* of the United Methodist Church is typical [I refer several times to the United Methodist Church because I am a member of that denomination.]:

> The United Methodist Church, a fellowship of believers, is a part of the Church Universal. Therefore all persons, without regard to race, color, national origin, or economic condition, shall be eligible to attend its worship services, to participate in its programs, and, when they take the appropriate vows, to be admitted into its membership in any local church in the connection.[33]

In the United Methodist Church then, the general ministry of the church is available to the homosexual person, but membership is contingent on appropriate vows.

# Q

**Should individuals who engage in homosexual behavior take membership vows?**

# A

The church's membership vows include an affirmation of faith in God, confession of Jesus Christ as Lord and Savior, profession of the Christian faith as contained in the Scriptures, and the promise "according to the grace given them to live a Christian life and always remain faithful members of Christ's holy Church."[34] The United Methodist *Discipline* further affirms that homosexual persons, no less than heterosexual persons, are persons of sacred worth. They need the ministry and guidance of the church and the spiritual and emotional care that the fellowship of the church can offer. However, the United Methodist Church's stance that homosexual practice is incompatible with the Christian life is made clear by this statement: "We do not condone the practice of homosexuality and consider this practice incompatible with Christian teaching."[35] (This is generally true in other mainline church bodies.) This determines the direction of ministry the church may offer a homosexual person. To hold otherwise is to believe Jesus Christ justifies sin rather than the sinner.

If, on the other hand, the homosexual person is willing to repent of his or her sins and take the vows of membership as all other repentant sinners are expected to do, he or she should be admitted into the membership of the church. When that occurs, all the resources of the church are made available to him or her.

# Q
**If a homosexual person accepts Christ, does he or she no longer have homosexual desires?**

# A
Repentance and conversion to Jesus Christ does not normally free one from homosexual urges. The homosexual orientation remains and may continue to plague the Christian homosexual person. That being the case, ministry to the homosexual person will take the form of helping that person either to convert to a heterosexual orientation and perhaps marriage or else to live a celibate life. If God's prescription for the life of a disciple prohibits homosexual practice, we need to have the faith to believe that one or the other of these options will be attainable to the homosexual person by means of God's grace. Through two millenniums millions of single Christians have demonstrated that the celibate life is possible.

# Q
**Is it possible for a homosexual to change his or her sexual orientation?**

# A
Conversion to a heterosexual lifestyle may not be practically attainable by all homosexual persons. Nevertheless, this alternative should be offered as a possibility for anyone caught in the grips of homosexuality. Even John McNeill, one of the founders of the New York chapter of Dignity, the organization of Catholic homosexual persons, writes:

> Practically all authorities agree that the first goal of counseling should be to guide the person with a homosexual problem to a heterosexual adjustment whenever possible.
>
> The person who merely fears he may be a homosexual, or is attracted to the homosexual community, should explore every avenue toward the achievement of normal heterosexual capacities and relationships.[36]

The availability of God's grace for such a conversion is implicit in all the general scriptural promises of victory over sin and deliverance from its power. There is also an explicit promise in Paul's reference to deliverance from the sin of homosexuality in 1 Corinthians 6:11: "That is what some of you were. But you were washed, you were sanctified, you were justified in the name of the Lord Jesus Christ and by the Spirit of our God." God is no respecter of persons. If He gave grace to the Corinthians for this particular need, He will do so for others with the same need. Certainly hope is greater for such a change if the subject is a Christian and has the support of the church. In that instance the Holy Spirit empowers the person from within, and the body of Christ lends external support through contacts and relationships.

## Q

**How difficult is it for the person with homosexual desires to change?**

## A

The informed pastor can probably help the average young person who is struggling for identity and who may suspect he/she is a homosexual but has not been involved in ho-

mosexual practice. However, helping the confirmed homosexual change to a heterosexual orientation requires the help of a qualified therapist, pastoral or otherwise.

Bieber and others note that age, extent and duration of homosexual practice, motivation, guilt and other factors affect a favorable prognosis. Motivation is particularly important since change involves struggle. This is true because of the depth of the problem and because homosexual practice satisfies fulfillment of normal sexual urges.

## Q

**What is the goal of therapeutic approaches to homosexual behavior?**

## A

We cannot here consider all the various therapeutic approaches to helping the homosexual person cope with his/her sexual urges or convert them to a heterosexual orientation. However, we might note briefly that at least one goal is common to all therapeutic approaches, except perhaps behavioral approaches and pharmacological approaches. That goal is what Nouwen has referred to as self-availability.[37] Relating to oneself meaningfully always requires being available to self. This is then a common task in all therapy, a ruthless kind of self-honesty that enables one to become aware of one's true feelings consciously and unconsciously. This is contrary to our normal way of relating to ourselves in our efforts to appear in an acceptable light, even at the cost of self-deception. Self-honesty is absolutely essential for the homosexual person in therapy, for it is only as one becomes aware of one's true feelings that moral choices can be made regarding those feelings. On the other hand, denying essential feelings will result in harm. Nouwen affirms:

The gospel makes it overwhelmingly clear that Christ came to reveal man's real condition in all its greatness as well as misery and to challenge man to face it without fear. Christ invited man to take off the mask of his illusion of self-righteousness.

He in no way judges feelings or emotions. He only asks us not to deny, distort, or prevent them, but to make them available for God's love.[38]

Acknowledging feelings also robs them of their compulsive power.

There are similarities in the therapeutic approach described above and what Robert Kronemeyer calls "Syntonic Therapy." As to the effectiveness of that therapy, Kronemeyer claims, "About eighty percent of homosexual men and women in Syntonic Therapy have been able to free themselves and achieve a healthy and satisfactory heterosexual adjustment . . . ."[39]

**Q**

**How can we best meet homosexual persons' individual needs?**

**A**

Meaningful and supportive relationships and what Harvey calls a plan of life can help to meet these common needs of homosexual persons. The body of Christ can offer a supportive relationship as a group, and the trained pastor can offer a strong relationship in the counseling setting. The life plan is, however, an individual matter. Harvey's suggested life plan for the homosexual person endeavoring to live the Christian life includes daily meditation, corporate worship as often as possible, daily examination of conscience with stress on purification of motives, systematic reading of Holy Scripture, a carefully chosen confessor and guide and involvement in works of charity.[42] Such a life plan affords value to *anyone* when adapted to his/her own faith perspective.

## Q

**What can homosexuals themselves do to help others struggling with homosexual desires?**

## A

Harvey suggests that homosexuals who desire to live a chaste life should form a "Homosexuals Anonymous" group.[43] He notes that homosexuals in therapy benefit from association with other homosexuals. He believes, further, a "Homosexuals Anonymous" organization could offer support not available in any other context. He grants the reality of the temptation and the moral danger of such involvement. But he notes, "Surely the dangers faced by most isolated, or noncommunicating, homosexuals are greater."[44] This is an interesting approach, obviously similar in potential structure to that of Alcoholics Anonymous and deserving further consideration by the church.

## Q

**How can we minister to the families of homosexual individuals?**

## A

It may be necessary to help the person with the homosexual orientation communicate his/her circumstances to his/her family. This is not an easy task, but it can be made more bearable if an understanding pastor is involved in the process.

This being done, it will nearly always be necessary to help parents deal with personal feelings about their son or daughter. Guilt is often one of the first reactions. Parents will assume that their child's condition is somehow related to moral failure in parental relationships. It is helpful if parents can be shown that many factors may cause homosexuality. It is reasonably certain that no one factor can be pointed to as the sole cause. Parents also need help in seeing that all children bear the scars of inadequate parenting. Although the scars of homosexuality may appear more shameful to them, they are, nevertheless, no more grievous than those many children bear. However, the emotional reaction to homosexual practice is often stronger than reaction to other sins.

## Q

**How important is it that homosexuals feel acceptance from their families?**

## A

Parents should be helped to see also that they need to accept their son or daughter and endeavor to understand him or her. Only such openness can give the homosexual person the vital family support that can help him or her work through the problems associated with sexual orientation. Such family acceptance and understanding may require considerable pastoral care. Parents usually find it very difficult to respond positively to their homosexual child's needs. But acceptance for the homosexual person who has revealed his/her identity is extremely important. Rejection may only compound the problem. Howard Brown reports:

> Every year hundreds of disowned or runaway homosexual adolescents turn up at the office of the National Gay Task Force in New York City, looking for food, shelter, jobs; hundreds more roam the streets, keeping themselves alive by working as male prostitutes.[45]

## Q

**What role does guilt play in the homosexual's desire to change?**

## A

Bergler and others believe that the guilt that a person may feel in regard to his/her homosexuality can be beneficial if its energies are mobilized in the therapeutic process. Traditionally, the church has been adept at raising guilt, sometimes falsely. However, those endeavoring to minister to the homosexual should heed the warnings of McNeill, Szaz and others who suggest that needless misery can afflict the homosexual person when a sense of guilt is overstimulated. In all probability, those coming to a minister with this problem are already suffering more guilt feelings than they can handle. It seems more appropriate, therefore, to refrain from adding to that burden. Instead, we should offer the grace of forgiveness that God gives through faith in Jesus Christ and His atonement for sins.

## Q

**Is every homosexual person who becomes a Christian released from homosexual bondage?**

## A

No. We must be careful not to create unrealistic hope about the process of converting to heterosexuality. The facts are that not every homosexual person who becomes a Christian is delivered from his or her homosexual impulses. Many are, but we must face the reality that God does not always choose to deliver us from our infirmities—physical or psychological. Paul's experience with his thorn in the flesh, whatever it was, is a case in point. Conversion to a heterosexual orientation, then, may not be possible for everyone. It is certain, however, that God has promised that His grace is sufficient for us. His strength is made perfect in our weakness. His Spirit intercedes for us regarding our infirmities with groanings too deep to be uttered. Jesus Christ sits at the right hand of the Father in-

terceding on our behalf. And in the final analysis, "If God is for us, who can be against us?" (Rom. 8:31). Therefore, even though we cannot give certainty about deliverance from the infirmity, we can give assurance of God's strength to cope with it.

## Q

**Is everyone who has a homosexual experience a homosexual?**

## A

No. John R. Powell perceptively cautions about diagnosing a person as homosexual:

Many young men not having accurate information about homosexuality as either a condition or a behavior erroneously diagnose themselves as homosexual. Such a misdiagnosis can set in motion a self-fulfilling prophecy that is consummated by tapping into the biologically rooted possibilities for bisexuality which otherwise would probably be passed over developmentally without difficulty.[46]

What is needed, therefore is an accurate understanding of sexuality. Homosexual experimentation may be a common experience of children and adolescents that does not indicate a true homosexual orientation at all.

# Q

**Isn't it difficult to accept a homosexual while at the same time affirming the biblical injunction against homosexual behavior?**

# A

Yes. There is tension between a moral approach to ministering to the homosexual person on the one hand and the need for unconditional acceptance of that person on the other. But the moral approach is the most caring, ironically, because it allows the person receiving ministry to make choices.

Sims notes that because homosexuality appears to be an adaptive step that is taken unconsciously by a threatened personality for its own protection, there are those who claim that it is immovable, fixed as a part of one's being. Sims states further, however, that even Freud believed that a deviant act involved responsibility on the part of the actor. If this were not so, therapy could not help anyone. Therapy involves helping the person see that he/she is not a victim of circumstances. Past choices have something to do with present plight, and past and present choices govern in large measure the direction of one's life in the future. Sims then comments:

Therapy that does not rest upon such an assumption must necessarily rest upon some other, which would be empty of moral content unless it held a person responsible for choices. Without moral content therapy is simply manipulative. It cannot respect the critical ingredient of moral freedom as expressing every human being's unique individuality. The important thing to notice here is that an amoral psychotherapy that seeks to absolve the sufferer from moral responsibility is not only anti-Christian, it is actually heretical to orthodox Freudian assumptions. Christian theology and Freudian psychoanalytic theory agree here. What this argument leads to is that unless the church is ready to challenge homosexual claims about the normalness of homosexuality, then the church in effect joins in reducing and degrading the humanity of the very people to whom the church needs to minister.[47]

Homosexuality is only symptomatic of deeper needs. These deeper needs relate to self-esteem and self-worth which are only nurtured in relationships and environments where one feels understood and accepted. That the church can play a critical role in this process, providing the moral issue is settled, is indicated by the following statement by McNeill:

Logically, by his calling and his profession the clergyman should be the person to whom the homosexual could turn with complete confidence. And very often—some authors estimate at least forty percent of the time—the clergyman is the first person to whom he turns and reveals his problem. If, however, the homosexual should fail to receive a sympathetic reception, which unfortunately often seems to be the case, ' could easily lose all .

n the other hand, the very fact of being able to speak openly about his problem for the first time with a respected member of the community, who continues to manifest respect for him, can be an essential step toward establishing hope, where previously there was only despair.[48]

## Q

**Does the church have the opportunity to address issues related to homosexuality that affect the entire community?**

## A

Yes. One issue with which the church must concern itself is the homosexual's civil rights. That homosexual persons are being treated with prejudice and deprived of civil rights in some instances is beyond question. Jones cites the case of a soldier who, having homosexual impulses and fearing that he might become a practicing homosexual, sought the aid of a military psychiatrist. Instead of help, he received an undesirable discharge and his military service record became a hindrance for some time.[49] Busby tells of a Baptist preacher from California who sought his help for overt homosexuality. This man said he was jailed in Evanston and confined with rapists and narcotic addicts. He reported that the police "glibly played cards with these other men, whereas they would hardly even speak with him and would push his food tray to him with their foot or even with a pole!"[50] Reports of such incidents could be multiplied thousands of times over. It is an undisputable fact that homosexual persons are deprived of some of their rights because of the prejudice of society toward the nature of their problem. These issues are discussed in more detail in chapter four in this book. We mention them here as an example of areas where the church should be ministering.

# Q

**What should the church do when homosexuals' civil rights conflict with the rights of others?**

# A

The issues are complex. There is often a conflict between the interests and needs of the homosexual person as an individual and the interests and needs of the community.

Greenlee explores a Dade County dilemma about the issue of whether a homosexual person has the right to teach in a public school:

If a person whose standards of conduct differ from those of the community wishes to apply for a teaching position, so long as his actual conduct and words do not clash with those principles, he may have the right to seek such a position, at least in a public school. However, if an applicant or a group of applicants declares openly to be significantly opposed to the standards considered acceptable by the school board and the parents of the community and demand acceptance *on that basis,* then it is no longer a matter of the applicant's civil rights, but rather the civil rights of the organization and of its members to maintain their organization and its purposes.[51]

This tension between individual and community rights does not excuse the church from involvement. The church has traditionally been the defender of both and is obligated to wrestle with the many issues involved in the quest for civil rights of homosexual persons and of our institutions.

## Q

**How does the emergence of the AIDS disease relate to our ministry efforts?**

## A

The AIDS crisis, which is discussed in chapter one of this book, presents an unprecedented challenge to the church during this age. Since at first the disease was primarily transmitted by male homosexuals and IV drug users, it is the church's tendency to see AIDS as a homosexual disease. However, " . . . the HIV virus, which causes AIDS, knows nothing of homosexuality or drug abuse. It is a dumb virus. And it can be passed to anyone. . . ."[52] Nevertheless, two trends are already in motion which will sabotage the church's efforts to meet the challenge of the AIDS virus.

On the one hand there is the temptation for those in the church who wish to see practicing homosexuals accepted into the church at all levels, including membership and ordination, to use the AIDS issue to champion their cause. That was the case at the "National Consultation on AIDS Ministries" held in San Francisco in November, 1987—a consultation sponsored by the United Methodist Church. In spite of an early declaration in the conference that AIDS is not a "gay" disease, some of the program speakers and recognized guests encouraged directly or by inference the practice of homosexuality.

On the other side of the fence are those who see AIDS as God's punishment and just reward for those who practice homosexuality. Their condemnation blinds them to the threat of this "dumb virus" to all society.

In spite of the fact that in our nation to date the male homosexual community has been at highest risk for AIDS, the church must approach these as two separate issues if we are to meet either with creative intervention. Though related incidentally, AIDS and homosexuality are not synonymous issues.

## Q

**Has the church itself done anything to encourage homosexuality?**

## A

Some factors do suggest that

as an agent of society the church has played some role in the promotion of homosexuality. Most citizens of the United States at one time or another have contact with the church. For that reason alone, the church must accept some responsibility for the prevalence of homosexuality, either by default or by direct contribution. Also, unquestionably there are many homosexual persons in the church. Those who counsel in Christian college and seminary communities find themselves dealing with a significant number of persons with homosexual problems. On the average Christian college campus, a chapel address that deals at all compassionately with the problem of homosexuality will nearly always bring a flood of persons to the counseling room for help. Counselors in such a setting sometimes wonder if the incidence of homosexuality is not greater on the Christian college campus than on its secular counterpart.

There are also some studies that indicate there are proportionately more homosexual persons among the clergy than in society in general. Jones quotes the statistics of one study that indicated that "of 4,040 sex variants studied, 1.6 percent were clergymen, while only 0.2 percent of the total male population are clergymen."[53] Simple mathematics suggests that the proportion of homosexual males in the ministry is eight times greater than in the population as a whole.

Personality tests show that male seminary students score noticeably higher on measures of effeminacy than do their secular professional peers. Although these measurements do not necessarily indicate homosexuality, they do suggest that male ministers present a more effeminate role model than does the average male.

Let us be quick to declare that these suspicions and limited statistics cannot produce clear conclusions. But they should lead us to ask what role the church has in promoting or attracting homosexuality. It would be ironic indeed to discover that the church is unknowingly, but directly, contributing to a problem with which it is critically engaged at this time. To this writer's knowledge, no studies have been done in this area.

The church's repressive attitude toward sexuality over the centuries and the unfortunate taboos that have resulted contribute to the explosive power of sex in our society.

**Q**

**Is it also possible that the role relationship between men and women in the church and its programs also may contribute to causing homosexuality?**

**A**

There seems to be no question but that the role relationship between men and women in the church varies from that of society as a whole. Through abdication by males, for whatever reason, the female is the more active leader in the church as a whole.

**Q**

**In light of these theories, what can the church do to curb individuals' attraction to homosexuality?**

**A**

On the constructive side, the church can do some things that may help prevent homosexuality, at least to the extent that it is caused by psychological factors.

Some claim the church has not changed its views on sexuality since the Middle Ages and that it has in fact ignored all subsequent data. This observation probably has some validity. Some persons in the church, however, *are* beginning to examine the knowledge coming from the behavioral sciences to see what light it may shed on a Christian understanding of sexuality. This kind of pursuit needs to continue. Those of the Christian community who have the knowledge and the gifts—the biblically trained psychologist, psychiatrist, pastoral counselor and social worker—should take the initiative in sponsoring such studies. We have long been too defensive about knowledge from the secular fields. It is high time we demonstrate faith and confidence in the revelation we claim as authority and realize that it will stand without our defensive posturings. Such a faith and confidence in the Bible would allow us to be more open to truth coming through other channels.

The church must also take a more prominent role in sex education. Too often the church has criticized and resisted sex education in our society. Only when it became obvious that sex education was going to come whether the church wanted it or not did the church begin to get involved. The church still lags far behind, however.

**Q**

**Is there a uniquely Christian view of sexuality?**

**A**

Yes. If we believe that there is a Christian perspective on what constitutes the good life, then we believe there is a Christian perspective on sexuality. If we believe other views are deficient or limited, then it behooves us to proclaim the Christian view. There is a Christian view of sexuality, a view that holds that a person is body, mind and spirit. Any complete view of sexuality must consider that holistic perspective, because sex involves body, mind and spirit. The biblical concept of one-fleshness and sexuality is the only perspective that leads to an exalted interpretation of sexuality and to complete fulfillment. Other views that reduce sex to the level of the sensual rob it of its true essence and the potential it has to serve God and humanity, not only in procreative ways but also in recreative ways. The church should be leading those responsibly endeavoring to educate society about its sexu-

ality. Such education should issue from the pulpit, the church classrooms, the home and anywhere else the church has an audience.

**Q**

**How should the church approach teaching on sexuality?**

**A**

Even the experts are not certain whether persons are innately heterosexual, innately heterosexual and homosexual, innately homosexual or born neutral in their sexual identity. Most experts suspect that sexual identity is a learned response or, even if it is innate or predisposed, can be skewed by the learning process. This leads Hiltner to comment:

If you wish all persons to emerge in adolescence and adulthood with a dominantly heterosexual orientation, then you must study the complex factors that reinforce such an orientation and support them, while you also study the forces that lead to a dominantly homosexual orientation and attempt to decrease them.[54]

This suggests that the educational role of the church relates not only to sexuality in general but also to identifying and presenting models that lead to the formation of heterosexual identity. There is a need to induce positive learning toward heterosexuality and to limit learning in the direction of homosexuality. Calderone echoes this concern when she states, "Education for heterosexuality involves far more than education about the processes of reproduction or of physical mating; it most importantly is education about the roles of and relationships between men and women."[55] She maintains that we can no longer take a passive stance in regard to this educational process:

> We can no longer depend on old patterns or "inborn" drives or on the simplistic moralistic negatives of our fathers to achieve the goals we want. It is no longer even possible to trust the "instincts" of mothers and fathers to come through in the creation of the kind of stable family milieu that we used to look to for the production of stable human beings.[56]

The church has made, and is continuing to make, a concerted effort to present scriptural teaching about marriage and the family. This effort is vital and merits even more attention as we continue to try to understand Scripture in the light of current findings on sexuality. Marriage and family relationships receive considerable treatment in both Testaments and, as Powell has observed, "all combine to suggest a model of family life and child development which is the antithesis of many findings in the family patterns of homosexually oriented males."[57] Thus, the church with its resources of revelation is in a unique position to teach and model roles and relationships for wholesome sexuality.

# Q

**Does the church have useful tools to help those struggling with homosexuality?**

# A

One model that the church could uphold is the witness of Christian homosexual persons who have either been able to convert to a heterosexual lifestyle or have been victorious in living a chaste life. Such persons no doubt abound, and their witness could be of immeasurable encouragement as well as profitable instruction to others struggling with the problem. The church has long known the power of personal witness and so should elicit more such testimony from those who have found God's grace to be sufficient in this particular area of weakness. Naturally, there will be no such witness as long as the church reacts to homosexuality with unforgiving, loathsome contempt. As Paul indicates, homosexuality is on a par with greed, envy, deceitfulness, gossiping, slander and other such sins common to us all (Rom. 1:26-31).

# Q

**How can the church assume a leadership role in the issue of homosexuality?**

# A

The church first must do some in-depth and ruthless soul-searching before it presumes to proclaim the answers in this area. The church must confess its own complicity in the problem and the destructive attitudes it has held. The church must proclaim with love its acceptance of all persons, regardless of the nature of their personal struggles, and guard against any appearance of self-righteousness. That will probably require a radical conversion of self-awareness on the part of the church with a sensitive ear to those condemnations of her by those of opposing positions. Their criticisms may not be accurate, but the opinions of one's opponents often contain a modicum of truth. The ability to hear those criticisms, therefore, can help the church respond to the issues involved in endeavoring to minister to the problem of homosexuality.

There is also the danger that fear of the struggle with issues surrounding homosexuality will immobilize the church. Some fear homosexuality will divide the church. Others fear it won't. In any event, the Christian is required to believe that God can act creatively in the midst of conflict and that in coming to grips with the issues of homosexuality, the church will experience new depths of spiritual maturity and certainty of the grace promised to it in the Christian gospel. As long as the church finds its authority in the Scriptures and as long as Christians endeavor to follow its admonitions, they will experience the good life and have opportunity to lead others in their pursuits of it. Jesus

Christ gave His life that humankind might have life more abundantly; He lives to lead His people.

A colleague of mine had a way of putting issues into proper perspective. On one occasion we were discussing the persons and issues involved in a conflict we faced which was seemingly caused by others. "Well, I guess I'll just have to get closer to the Lord," he commented. That is precisely the challenge the church faces as it addresses itself to the issues related to homosexuality and develops a ministry to the persons involved.

# 6

# Medical and Psychological Evidence on Homosexuality

## William P. Wilson

"Are homosexuals born that way?" and "Can homosexuals change?" are two questions asked over and over by counselors, ministers and laypersons. The medical world has produced a blizzard of detailed, sometimes contradictory evidence attempting to answer these questions. The following chapter is a serious, in-depth look at that evidence. People who want the facts will appreciate Dr. Wilson's careful research.

### Q

**Why do most people consider homosexuality an abnormal behavior?**

### A

Normal males and females are unmistakably different. They differ from each other physically, endocrinologically, physiologically, psychologically and behaviorally. "Biological intent is to differentiate males and females. . .in such a manner as to insure species survival which can be served only through heterosexual union."[1] God as Author of nature designed man and woman as

*William P. Wilson is Professor of Psychiatry emeritus, former Head of the Division of Biological Psychiatry at Duke University Medical Center, Durham, North Carolina. He is a graduate of Duke University, B.S., and Duke University School of Medicine, M.D., and is a Research Fellow in Medicine in the Department of Psychiatry and Medicine at Duke Medical School, a Resident in Psychiatry at Duke Medical School and a Fellow in EEG, Montreal Neurological Institute in Montreal, Canada. He is head of the Institute of Christian Growth, Burlington, North Carolina .*

companions whose complementariness would provide an appropriate setting where new individuals could grow to maturity and thus continue the species. Homosexuality is therefore a deviation from what is normal and as such has been studied throughout recorded history.

# Q

**Do scientists believe homosexuality is caused by biological or psychological factors?**

# A

With the development of modern science, early investigations of homosexuality concentrated on the physical workings of the body. Both Krafft-Ebing and Havelock-Ellis[2] believed that homosexuality has a constitutional, or hereditary, cause. However, the development of Freudian dynamic psychiatry caused an abrupt shift from this position to an emphasis on early-life experiences as the primary cause. W.J. Gadpaille noted that two distinct theoretical positions exist—biological and environmental. The first claims an inborn biological sexuality. In this view a child's development proceeds through a series of stages. Some of the phases are more difficult than others for the child to complete successfully, depending on his/her constitutional make up. The second theory finds "a typical family constellation in the background of male homosexuals, consisting of a close, intimate, binding mother and a detached, indifferent or hostile father. The mother's influence demasculinizes the son and strips the father of admirable masculine qualities, and the father makes identification with himself unpalatable."[3] The converse is true for female homosexuals. This latter theoretical model has gained the most support from studies of male and female homosexuals.

Those who accept the second theory, however, face a problem. It is very difficult to change the sexual object choice of the homosexual. Equally difficult to explain are the behavioral variations observed in some of these individuals.[4] These behavioral differences are so profound that even when one believes homosexuality has its origin in early life experiences, one may nevertheless suspect that in time a cause will be found in the inner workings of the body.

Animal studies that suggest that the brain not only determines the endocrinal differences between the sexes[5] but also controls to some degree the behavioral differences[6] reinforce this doubt. It is, therefore, impossible to ignore research that has investigated the genetic and hormonal aspects of both normal and abnormal human sexual behavior.

# Q

**Why should we review the differences between normal male and female sexual behavior when studying abnormal sexual behavior?**

# A

Corinne Hutt, reviewing the literature about early life development in the behavior of males and females,[7] notes that some authors believe boys and girls are the same at birth and that they adjust to their sex assignment irrespective of their actual hormonal or genetic sex.[8] This idea is advanced because hermaphrodites (persons whose external sexual apparatus is not appropriate for their sex hormone secreting glands) who are often anatomically masculinized females or feminized males adopt the attitudes, opinions, dress and mannerisms of their assigned sex. This, however, is not the same as *role adoption*[9] which relates to observable sex-related behaviors such as activity levels, exploratory behavior and nurturing attentiveness. Biological factors should affect the latter, especially in the homosexual. The interrelatedness of role identification, role adoption and sexual object choice suggests we study the differentiation of normal sexual behavior in early life to better understand the anomalies.

# Q

**How much sexual differentiation begins before birth?**

# A

Space does not permit us to review in detail the sexual differentiation of the unborn child (fetus). However, we should mention a few facts about this differentiation. The first is the importance of the Y (male) chromosome (see explanation on page 141 in the determination of maleness). The Y chromosome causes differentiation as a male (except when the cells of the developing child are insensitive to male sex hormones).

This is true even when one or more extra X (female) chromosomes are present. Once the fetal male sex glands (testes) are formed, they secrete testosterone, the male sex hormone that causes the development of male sex organs (genitalia). As the fetus develops, testosterone also causes a differentiation of its brain into that of a male. This occurs in an area at the base of the brain called the hypothalamus, resulting in a cyclic secretion of hormone in the female, while that of the male is acyclic. The hypothalamus controls the secretion of hormones by the pituitary gland which in turn controls all other hormone-secreting glands in the body, including the ovaries and the testes. Two areas of the hypothalamus control secretion of these hormones. One governs the tonic, or continuous, secretion. The other governs the cyclic, or periodic, secretion; this area of the hypothalamus, called the preoptic nucleus, is larger in the female.[10] The hypothalamus also plays a part in controlling drives and emotional behavior.

# Q

**Does sexual differentiation continue after birth?**

# A

Yes. Continuing development brings further physical differentiation.[11] At birth males exceed females in both weight and length. Males have a higher metabolic rate and a higher caloric intake. Males are slightly more active than females in total motor activity. Their motor behavior is also quite different in that male activity consists of grosser movements.

Studies of mother-infant interaction reveal a significant difference between males and females. Male infants are more irritable than females, and therefore they receive significantly more interaction. This seems to be less true at older ages, though mothers continue to stimulate male children more. These interactional differences seem to be the outcome of behavior that is occurring because of the sex of the child.

As children grow older, obvious sex-related differences in behavior continue. Males are less reluctant to leave their mothers and are less fearful. They are more likely to seek solutions to problems. Males are more aggressive, both displaying and eliciting aggression. Competition also is stronger in males.

# Q

## What are some of the causes of this differentiation?

# A

Aggressive behavior in the human is linked to the presence of the male sex hormone during the development of the fetus. Supporting this statement are many observations that females display more aggressive behavior when they have been exposed *in utero* to masculinizing hormones. This exposure may result from a defect in cortisone metabolism (a hormone produced in the adrenal glands) or when large doses of progestin (a normal female hormone that has some masculinizing effects) are given to prevent miscarriage. In contrast to the observation that males are more aggressive is the observation that cooperation is a more feminine trait. Most studies have demonstrated that females display a remarkable degree of nurturing attentiveness early in life. Also, males and females have a great tendency to interact predominantly with members of their own sex.

Males are far more exploratory than females and are considered to be more creative. Whether this is related to intelligence differences is not clear, but research shows that males are superior in reasoning or the logical manipulation of concepts, regardless of whether the content of the problem is expressed in numbers, words or patterns.

In her summary on human sex differentiation, Hutt explains that "genetic complements confer special properties on the course of development, but gonadal hormones, and the testicular hormones in particular, have important formative and organizational functions. From the moment of birth onwards, differences in structures, in metabolism, in physiological and psychological functions characterize the development of the two sexes." She concludes by stating that the sex-related developmental similarities between monkeys, chimpanzees and children make a purely environmental interpretation of normal sex differences difficult to accept.[12] Although her article was published in 1973, no evidence has accumulated in the last 15 years to refute her assertions.

# Q

## How do genes affect human development?

# A

The reproductive cells of every species of animal contain material carrying the appearance, life functions and, to some extent, the behavior of every member of that species. Human cells hold about 3,000,000,000 bits. This material divides at certain stages of cell development into chromosomes. Each chromosome is made up of many smaller bits. These are called genes. The male reproductive cell (sperm) and the female (ovum) each carries one-half of the material necessary to form a complete cell that can develop into an adult animal. Because many divisions occur in the development of the reproductive cells, errors can occur. Sometimes divisions take place that leave the developing sperm or ovum with too many or too few chromosomes of a particular kind. When any of these reproductive cells with an abnormal chromosome complement are involved in creating a fetus, the chromosomal abnormality is lethal to development. If there are too many or too few sex chromosomes, the cell does not die, but develops into a person with a congenital irregularity.

Other diseases result from the organization of the building blocks of the genes. These abnormalities are not lethal but instead give rise to such diseases as high blood pressure, diabetes or certain kinds of epilepsy, to name a few. It is believed that some behavior is also in part determined by the structure of the genes.

# Q

**Since evidence indicates that sexual behavior in normal humans is partially genetically determined, does evidence also suggest that homosexuality has a genetic basis?**

# A

The obvious place to begin searching for an answer is to examine studies of identical and fraternal twins and persons with sex chromosome abnormalities.

F.J. Kallman's report in 1952 that homosexuality in 40 identical twin pairs affected both of the twins similarly has recently been refuted.[13] Kallman's data have always been highly criticized, especially because there should have been a high incidence of homosexuality among first order relatives of the twins. There was not! Second, most of the twins were mentally ill with schizophrenia or had severe personality problems. The fact that they were mentally ill distorts the patient population. Third, the twins were not reared apart, suggesting that environmental factors could have been just as significant as their genetic similarity. It is therefore impossible to draw any conclusions from Kallman's data. The more recent work of Eckert et al. found no corresponding sexual preference among identical twins (two male pairs and four female pairs) reared apart. He also reviewed the literature since Kallman's work and discovered a high incidence of dissimilar twins in other studies, even when the twins were reared in the same environment. He concluded that one cannot attribute homosexuality to genetic factors.

# Q

**What do studies of people with abnormal numbers of sex chromosomes reveal?**

# A

Such studies shed some light on the determination of sexual behavior and preferences.[14] Men with Klinefelter's syndrome have an extra female chromosome (XXY, two female and one male chromosome) and have an increased incidence of homosexuality and transvestism (dressing like the opposite sex). Individuals with this syndrome are anatomically male, but their genitalia may not enlarge at puberty and their body build may be eunuchoid (female), with breast development. Their testes are usually small and do not produce sperm. Their sex drive is low, and sexual activity, if it occurs, is infrequent.

The XYY syndrome, in which there is an extra male chromosome, was initially thought to be always characterized by impulsiveness, aggression and violence. However, subsequent research has only partly corroborated these initial observations as not all cases manifest these traits. Homosexuality may occur in the XYY syndrome.

Turner's syndrome is characterized by an absence of the normal complement of sex chromosomes (XO). In individuals with this abnormality the internal reproductive structures do not form even though the external genitalia are female. In the absence of ovaries, puberty does not take place. Even so, these individuals are characteristically female. On psychological tests that differentiate masculine from feminine interests, females with Turner's syndrome have greater feminine interests than normal women. They are not reported to be homosexual.

## Q

**Do studies of these unusual conditions demonstrate that homosexual behavior is directly produced by genetically transmitted traits or by excessive or deficient numbers of sex chromosomes?**

## A

It is true that extra female or male chromosomes may influence behavior. Some speculate that in Klinefelter's syndrome the extra X chromosome interferes in some way with the normal organization of the brain that determines sexual behavior. This results in the decreased sex drive common in this problem. In the XYY syndrome, the organization of the brain may be changed to result in increased aggression in some persons. In the XO syndrome the absence of sex hormones, occurring because the ovaries fail to develop, gives rise to brain development that results in increased feminine behavior. It is possible that the

changes in Klinefelter's syndrome (XXY) and Turner's syndrome (XO) are entirely related to the hormonal deficiencies and are secondary to the genetic defects. The occurrence of homosexuality in Klinefelter's and the XYY syndrome cannot be related to the genetic defect or to hormonal changes since it occurs only occasionally.

Modern medicine has made rapid strides in the study of genetics. Scientists now have techniques to study genes at the molecular level. To this author's knowledge, none of these techniques has been used to investigate homosexuality or transsexuality. We do not know what the future may reveal in this exciting new area of research.

## Q

**How do hormones influence normal male/female development?**

## A

Two major biological differences exist between men and women. These are (1) the secretion of different sex hormones and (2) the cyclic secretion of the female sex hormones.

Animal behavior is profoundly influenced by the presence of androgens (hormones that have masculinizing effects) at critical times in the development of the fetus and throughout life. It has been suggested that nature's prime purpose is to produce females. Maleness results only from the effects of androgens. In the absence of androgens or androgen effects, the anatomical development and behavior of the female (XX) or male (XY) fetus will be female. Conversely, when active androgens are present, the development and behavior will be male. Even small quantities of androgens at appropriate points in the life of an animal fetus will cause the brain to develop so that the infant and adult animal will display behavior that is considered masculine. Human females may be masculinized because of a defect in adrenal steroid (cortisone) metabolism. This defect produces large quantities of androgenic hormones which cause their external sexual organs to appear masculine. It also affects the organization of the brain to produce a tendency toward masculine behavior. Females with this condition exhibit increased homosexual activity and inclination and respond to visual and narrative sexual stimuli with increased arousal, much as males have been reported to respond. This same observation has been made of women who had hermaphroditism induced by progestin, another hormone with masculinizing effects.

In contrast, some males have an androgen insensitivity syndrome. These males are born with a normal genetic complement (XY), but because of an inherited enzyme defect, the tissues of the developing fetus do not respond to secreted testosterone. These genetic males are born as perfectly normal-looking females. They are then reared as girls, and their condition is discovered only when they fail to menstruate. Investigation usually reveals that they are actually genetic males (XY). Their gender identity, assignment and rearing has, however, been unequivocally feminine. These individuals function quite well as females when appropriate surgery and hormonal administration is carried out. Gadpaille comments that "nature will differentiate a female in the absence of effective fetal androgen, and that chromosomal hormonal and gonadal sex is overridden by this female-first principle and by gender assignment and rearing."[15]

Q

**How do hormone imbalances in fetal life influence an individual's adult behavior?**

A

Clearly, hormones play a critical role in the development of external genitalia, as well as in determining adult sexual behavior. The critical time for the action of the hormones is in the first few months after conception, for it is then that the development of the testes and ovaries takes place. The presence of functional testes then determines the development of the external genitalia. This in turn influences gender assignment and rearing. Both of these factors are inseparably linked, so that hormonal disturbances in fetal life affect both the structure of the genitals and sexual behavior in later life. This knowledge is of critical importance as we evaluate the data obtained in biological studies of homosexuals.

Q

**What studies have been done to search for a possible biological cause of homosexuality?**

A

Most studies that have attempted to determine whether there is a biological basis for homosexuality have been conducted during the last 30 years. As we have noted, little evidence supports the notion that homosexuality is a genetically transmissible behavior. Neither genetic studies of identical twins, nor studies of genetic abnormalities support this possibility. Indeed, they tend to refute the hypothesis that such might be the case. Evidence does however support the *possibility* that hormonal influences could be the cause. Hormonal influences would be most likely to affect behavior during the period of developmental organization of the hypothalamic nuclei early in fetal life and in the remainder of the growth period prior to puberty.

Q

**Could a lack of testosterone before birth cause a male to have a female hypothalamus?**

A

If the organization of the hypothalamus is female, it *could* cause homosexuality in the male. If this is so, it should be possible to demonstrate a cyclic, female type of gonadotropin secretion in homosexuals. Gonadotropins are pituitary hormones that control the secretion of male and female sex hormones from the testes and ovaries. A cyclic pattern of secretion would result from the failure of the testes to secrete adequate quantities of testosterone during the early prenatal period. This would mean the homosexual's role adoption and sexual object choice is due to the hypothalamic maldevelopment that also gives rise to female gonadotropin release patterns. However, although studies by Halbreich and others do reveal significant day-to-day variations from normal, the average secretion rate was the same for homosexuals as for heterosexuals. There was no evidence of cyclic variation. The increased variation in daily secretion was thought possibly to be due to a deficiency of testosterone around the time of birth.[16] Careful inspection of the data of these authors does not reveal that the homosexuals' patterns of secretion could be considered female. The earlier work of Doerr et al. and Kolodny et al., as well as the very recent work of Gooren (who used unorthodox techniques), do not suggest that homosexuals have unusual gonadotropin secretion.[17]

# Q
**Could deficient testosterone secretion after birth cause homosexuality?**

# A
This theory is not supported by the work of several investigators. Loraine et al. and Kolodny et al. in 1971 did report lowered levels of testosterone and a high incidence of azoospermia (no sperm) in male homosexuals.[18] They postulated that these findings might be compatible with a possible biological predisposition to homosexuality. Neither Migeon nor Gooren were able to replicate these findings in regard to testosterone levels. Migeon actually found a high level in one subject.[19] Starka and other authors have also been unable to demonstrate low levels of testosterone in male homosexuals.[20] These studies do not relate abnormalities of gonadotropin and sex hormone secretion to homosexuality.

# Q
**But what about the study that found day-to-day varia-**

tions in the release of hormones between homosexual and heterosexual men? Doesn't this study show a biological cause of homosexuality?

**A**

The inconsistent variations in gonadotropin secretions may be due to the absence of ovaries in males to respond to a cyclic release. On the other hand, the low testosterone levels in adult life of some homosexuals may indicate an earlier deficiency that influenced the development of feminine behavior when the hypothalamic nuclei were not sufficiently stimulated to develop the male brain structure. However, the fact that some normal males and homosexuals have similar gonadotropin release patterns and similar low levels of testosterone lead to the conclusion that such hormonal disturbances do not cause males to be homosexual.

**Q**

What, if any, are the physiological differences between homosexuals and heterosexuals?

**A**

Physiological differences in ho-

mosexual males have seldom been reported. Zung and Wilson, who studied arousal from sleep, noted that normal females are significantly more arousable from sleep by auditory stimuli than are normal males in all stages of sleep except Rapid Eye Movement (REM).[21] Wilson and his coauthors compared the arousability of homosexual males to that of females and found a significant difference in the arousability from sleep of normal and homosexual males in the second, third and fourth stages of sleep.[22] No other studies have compared the physiological responses of normal and homosexual males and females except Masters and Johnson's studies of sexual physiology. They observed the physiology, functional efficiency, fantasy patterns and homosexual response patterns of a carefully selected group of male and female homosexual subjects. The physiological data they reported were obtained by observing subjects' responses to masturbation, partner manipulation and fellatio (oral sexual stimulation of the male) or cunnilingus (oral stimulation of the female). They found no functional efficiency differences between homo- or heterosexual men and women in response to similar sexual stimuli.[23]

**Q**

**Are there natural behavior differences between normal males and females that homosexuals lack that could indicate a behavioral abnormality is a cause of homosexuality?**

**A**

We noted earlier that Hutt listed a number of biologically determined behavioral differences that distinguish normal boys from normal girls. J. Money has a larger list that is quoted in Gadpaille. These are: (1) a higher energy expenditure in males; (2) differences in preferences in play, toys and sports; (3) boys prefer shirts, trousers, jeans etc.; (4) boys are less nurturant; (5) different career ambitions; (6) body image agrees with gender orientation; (7) visual and narrative perceptual erotic arousal patterns in the males.[24] However, little evidence exists to support all of Money's assertions. It is true that boys seem more active in the first few months of life, play more aggressively and are not nurturant, but no data suggests that dress preferences and career ambitions are not entirely determined by the culture. Also, recent evidence refutes the notion that men and women differ in perceptual erotic arousal.[25] There are no data to support or refute the other assertions in Money's statement.

**Q**

**Have any studies uncovered natural differences between homosexual and heterosexual individuals?**

**A**

A 15 year study of effeminate boys has revealed some significant differences in the childhood behavior of boys who at maturity became either transsexual or homosexuals. Green observed six variables that discriminated feminine boys from masculine boys. These were that effeminate boys: (1) either did cross dress or wanted to cross dress; (2) did not like to indulge in rough and tumble play; (3) wanted to be a girl; (4) did not want to be like their father; (5) paid attention to their mother's fashions; and (6) liked to play with dolls.[26] As with Money's list, it is obvious that some of the behaviors are likely to be culturally determined.

An added bit of evidence that basic sexual behavioral patterns are preserved in male and female homosexuals is the observation that they resemble their heterosexual brothers and sisters in their style of sexual affiliations. Male homosexuals seek sex for release and usually do not form long-term relationships, unlike lesbians, whose capacity for lasting relationships is similar to that of heterosexual women.[27]

## Q

**Have any medical remedies been shown to change sexual preference?**

## A

Medical treatments of homosexuality have not altered the sexual object choice of the homosexual. Even drugs and electric shock treatments given to these individuals for other psychiatric problems have caused no change of sexual preference, even when the psychiatric problem has been successfully treated. In contrast, psychological treatments have been reported by some authors to be quite successful in reorienting the homosexual to a normal object choice.[28] Such success adds more evidence against the possibility of a biological origin for the problem because biologically-determined mental disease is notoriously resistant to psychological interventions.

## Q

**If a physical origin of homosexuality is unlikely, do any studies suggest it is caused by psychological factors?**

## A

For many years the two major psychiatric explanations for homosexuality were that (1) the problem had a biological origin, or (2) it was due to the influence of a close, intimate, binding mother and a detached, indifferent or hostile father (or the converse for female children), which caused the child to identify with the opposite sex parent.[29] Conflicting with the analytic theory is the learning theory hypothesis proposed by Stoller, which has been severely criticized by Futuyma and Risch. They convincingly argue against the learning theory model. And Stoller himself, in a later work, uses anthropological evidence to refute his earlier assertions.[30] Although a dynamic sociopsychological origin is the most tenable hypothesis and has the most evidence to support it, the formulation as stated by Gadpaille is too simplistic. Homosexuality seems to be caused by many factors.

Moberly, in contrast to Socarides and Bieber, does not view the same sex parent as the primary "culprit," but found that disidentification with the same-sex parent is the primary problem. This seems to be a variation on the oedipal theme of Freud.[31] Further complicating the picture are Green's findings that effeminate behavior was manifest in young males who later became homosexual by the fourth year of life. A significant number of these boys displayed such behavior as early as the second year.[32] Such data suggests that the critical psychological events occurred in infancy, i.e. the first two years of extrauterine life.

## Q

**In your experience as a psychiatrist, what family scenarios have you seen give rise to homosexuality?**

## A

In three cases I have observed that a grandmother was the most likely "culprit." This is especially likely if the mother is ill or dominated by the grandmother. In another three cases the mother was severely depressed during the first two years of the patient's life and did not receive any help from other significant persons. In two of the three cases the father was absent most of the time so the mother had to care for the child while she was in a depressed state. In both instances the mother recovered and normal parent-child relationships were reestablished. In the other case the mother was psychotically depressed, but the family dynamics were such that homosexuality would probably have been the outcome under any circumstance.

## Q

**Do psychiatrists regard homosexuality as a mental illness?**

## A

The American Psychiatric Association has removed the diagnosis of homosexuality from the *Diagnostic and Statistical Manual of Mental Disorders*. This decision resulted from a vote of the members of the organization and pressure from gay activists (see page 152 for more details). It is unlikely that those voting made a decision based on new scientific evidence, for there is none. Most likely, the vote represented an acknowledgment of the extraordinary resistance of homosexuality to psychiatric intervention, the knowledge that most homosexuals' lives are relatively free of conflict and symptoms and a paucity of findings on psychological tests to demonstrate that homosexuals have significant psychopathology. Some passion and prejudice were involved in this decision as well.

# Q

**Do homosexuals have characteristic psychological problems?**

# A

Weinberg and Williams found that 68 percent of homosexuals had never received treatment for their homosexuality and 82 percent had no desire for treatment. Most homosexuals, according to their study, saw themselves as persons of worth and were satisfied with themselves. They had consistently good opinions of themselves and rarely got depressed. However, they did have more psychosomatic problems, tend-

ing to suffer from insomnia, anxiety, headache, gastrointestinal upsets and tremulousness. They often had nightmares and tended to abuse alcohol.

A sizable group seemed to be introverted, but about 50 percent felt quite good about their interpersonal relationships. Their "faith" in others seemed to indicate a high degree of trust.[33] Myers listed the common problems that homosexuals bring to the family physician; most prevalent are alcoholism, reactive depression, ego-dystonia, marriage difficulties, problems involving "coming out," specific sexual complaints, couple conflicts and medicolegal problems.[34]Unfortunately, no carefully controlled demographic studies of the psychological problems of homosexuals exist, except for studies of alcoholism and drug addiction among male and female homosexuals. These studies were recently summarized by Israelstam and Lambert, who reported a 30 percent incidence of alcohol and drug abuse among male homosexuals and a 40 percent incidence among lesbians. These are much higher rates (approximately 3 times for males and 20 times for females) than for the heterosexual population. They do comment, however, that although the studies that have been done produce consistent findings, larger and more in-depth studies are needed.[35]

Homosexuals' intelligence is slightly above normal in the studies of Raboch and Sipova.[36] Their data demonstrated a statistically significant artifact since there was a disparity in the size of their normal group and the sexually deviant groups.

# Q

**Are standard psychological tests able to differentiate homosexual from heterosexual individuals?**

# A

Psychological examinations of homosexuals designed to demonstrate psychopathology (extreme mental disorder) have not been rewarding. In 1957 Grygier summarized the literature and attempted to analyze the effectiveness of tests that had been administered to determine the feminine orientation of some homosexuals.[37] Tests such as the Minnesota Multiphasic Personality Inventory (MMPI), the California Personality Inventory

and the Guilford-Martin Inventory of Factors failed to differentiate homosexual from heterosexual men and women. The Terman-Miles test for masculinity and femininity gave better results but could not differentiate active homosexual males from normal males. In this instance "active" indicated those homosexuals who took a dominant role. Draw-a-person tests have also failed to differentiate adult homosexuals from heterosexuals, although effeminate boys who have taken the "It" Draw a Person and the Draw a Person test have shown significant differences.[38]

The Rorschach test does not differentiate men from women, nor do any responses differentiate the homosexual male from the normal male. The Thematic Apperception Test in the hands of a skilled clinician may be "satisfying," but when uniform scoring methods are used, they do not provide significant information regarding sexuality. The TAT does provide some increased understanding of the dynamics of homosexuality.

The Dynamic Personality Inventory revealed that homosexuals are more emotionally dependent and narcissistic and more frequently have a greater difference in masculinity and femininity scores. There was no mention of the incidence of psychopathology in Grygier's article.

Two studies by Siegelman inquired into the psychological adjustment of homosexual and heterosexual men.[39] To emphasize the depth of his studies, I have listed the wide variety of tests he used: the adjustment questionnaires of Schier and Catwell; the neuroticism questionnaire (NSQ); the alienation and trust measures of Streuning and Richardson; the Dignan scales of goal directedness, self acceptance and sense of self; a dependency test by Comry; a nurturance test by Haravey et al.; and the neuroticism measure by McQuire. Femininity was measured by the Gough Femininity Scale. Finally, he used the Crown-Marlowe Social Desirability Scale (SDS) and Socioeconomic Index.

Siegelman's results revealed that, when compared with heterosexual males, homosexuals were more submissive, tender-minded, anxious, nurturant and they had a greater sense of self. There was no difference in depression, alienation, trust, goal-directedness, self-acceptance and neuroticism. He divided his homosexual and heterosexual groups into those with low and high femininity scores. When he compared these groups, statistically significant differences were found only in the scores for nurturance in the low femininity group. In the high femininity group, tender-mindedness, self acceptance and nurturance were significantly different. He concluded that, in general, effeminate homosexuals were more neurotic than the heterosexual population. This was interpreted as being due to cultural pressures.

One of the earliest studies of homosexuals (1963) was that of Hooker. Her study used tests designed to demonstrate psychopathology. Using the MMPI, the TAT, the Rorschach Test and other psychological measures, she concluded that homosexuality is not necessarily and invariably an accompaniment to or symptom of psychopathology. After reviewing the relevant literature, she concluded that the only significant difference between homosexuals and heterosexuals is in psychosexual object choice. Gender identity does not seem to be disturbed.[40]

These studies show that no psychological profile will differentiate the homosexual from the heterosexual. In general the homosexual is neither unusually neurotic, nor is there evidence of severe personality disturbance. Currently available tests do not indicate a significant feminine orientation of male homosexuals, proving that gender identity and psychosexual object choice are independent of each other.

## Q

**Do homosexuals benefit from psychiatric treatment?**

## A

Although psychiatry has adopted the attitude that homosexuality is not a disease, psychiatrists still write about its treatment. In one of the standard textbooks of psychiatry, Marmor writes that although homosexuals present themselves for treatment— usually because of difficulty in attracting partners, break-up of relationships, problems of self-realization or various neuroses and depression—most of them simply want symptom relief. Others are unhappy with their sexual orientation and desire to function as heterosexuals.[41] This latter group are diagnosed as "ego-dys-

tonic" homosexuals. Some psychiatrists are treating this group with a goal of producing a reorientation of sexual object choice. Marmor reports a 20 to 50 percent success rate in this group.

## Q

**Psychologically, what impact has the emergence of AIDS had on homosexuals?**

## A

The occurrence of the Acquired Immune Deficiency Syndrome in the homosexual population has created several new psychiatric complications. For example, there is now a syndrome of AIDS phobia with symptoms of depression, self-pity, hopelessness and sometimes self-destructive tendencies. Homosexuals with this syndrome often view themselves as "toxic" to others. They see themselves as "lepers"— not because they have an illness, but because they are gay and at risk for AIDS. Guilt often disables them. They withdraw from social support systems. They are often angry in their frustration. They express this anger by directing it toward authority figures.[42] However, it is not clear that there has been an increase in ego dystonia as a result of the AIDS epidemic, so not many homosexuals are responding to the AIDS scare by seeking to become heterosexual.

The AIDS epidemic has also caused some homosexuals to deny the problem and to continue or even escalate their risk-taking behavior. Increased sexual activity is one means by which they alleviate their anxiety or depression.

## Q

**How do most mental health professionals approach the treatment of homosexuality?**

## A

Most modern psychiatrists and psychologists view homosexuality as a normal variation and treat other problems that may arise as the "disease." They consider ego dystonia a secondary problem of sexual orientation, and try to help the patient accept his or her homosexuality.

This view results from the development of a deterministic cosmology in the behavioral sciences.[43] Most persons in behavioral science have no belief in the supernatural and consider morality whatever man determines it to be. They see a homosexual as hopelessly trapped in his situation with no possibility of change.

## Q

**Do all psychiatrists accept this hopeless view of homosexuality?**

## A

No. Some have treated large numbers of homosexuals using a variety of techniques, and all have reported significant rates of successful reorientation. Individual psychotherapy has received the greatest attention because of the work of Bieber, Socarides, Ellis and Marmor.[44] Individual therapy may be carried out in conjunction with group therapy.[45] For the most part, therapists attempt to devalue homosexual impulses and actions while encouraging the patient to make heterosexual approaches. Socarides summarized the analytic treatment process as follows: it is necessary to interpret to the patient (1) his fear of castration, (2) his fear of oral dependency, (3) his disgust with the opposite sex and (4) his fear of his own destructiveness and sadism. Socarides reports that the interpretation that has proven most successful in relaxing homosexuals' resistance is to explain the homosexual's attempt to acquire masculinity or femininity through identification with the partner in the homosexual act. After achieving this insight, the patient may be able to function heterosexually.

Moberly's approach indirectly sees the core problem in a similar light. She postulates that the radical disidentification with the same-sex parent occurs in the homosexual as a result of the psychological separation of the child from the same-sex parent. The developing child, unable to obtain the auxiliary ego-strength needed to establish ego-boundaries, cannot extricate him/herself from the primary identification with the opposite-sex parent. As a result homosexuals have a radically incomplete psychological development. (Barnhouse also holds this view.)[46] They have not acquired the necessary masculinity or femininity because of the disidentification. Only when the dependency need for identification with the same-sex parent is met can therapy be successful. She is emphatic in her assertion that treatment cannot be successful if the therapist is of the opposite sex. Only through the process of transference (re-direction of unconscious childhood emotions) to a same-sex therapist can the person achieve the proper identification and thus become heterosexual.[47]

# Q

## What other treatments may be successful in reorienting a homosexual?

# A

Other types of therapy have been used successfully in the treatment of homosexuality. Hadden is group therapy's leading proponent.[48] Others have reported successful treatment in groups alone or combined with individual therapy.[49] All authors emphasize that to be successful the group should be homogenous.

The use of behavior therapy has been most adequately reviewed by Feldman and MacCullough.[50] Srnge and Freund have also used avoidance learning.[51] Aversion therapy establishes an aversion to the homosexual object choice by showing pictures of nude males when the patient is nauseated as a result of the administration of emetine. Others have applied electric shocks if the patient did not turn off the picture of a nude male in eight seconds. Immediately after the shock a picture of an attractive nude female was shown so that it could be associated with the relief of anxiety. Rekers has used positive reinforcement and extinction to treat effeminate males early in childhood in an effort to prevent the development of homosexuality in later life.[52] Masters and Johnson have also used behavioral therapy with good success, reporting results equal to those of other authors.[53]

# Q

**Have psychiatrists using a Christian approach been successful in helping homosexuals change their sexual orientation?**

# A

Christian psychotherapy has been reported to have helped homosexuals successfully reorient their sexual practices to heterosexuality.[54] The 10 cases reported were treated with a combination of individual and group psychotherapy. All were born-again Christians and were: (1) highly motivated, (2) repentant (John 5:3-6), (3) wanted to be transformed (Rom. 12:2), (4) had faith that God would transform them (Phil. 3:21), (5) were willing to state their case before God in prayer (James 5:13) and (6) wanted God's will for their lives (Luke 22:42). With this understanding, the authors were able to treat the patients with a variety of standard psychological interventions, as well as Christian interventions. The latter included prayer and confession, repentance and forgiveness. When they were available, the patients' families were also incorporated into the treatment, using standard family therapy techniques. The reported cases and a series of cases treated subsequently have a reorientation rate about equal to those reported by others (60%).

# Q

**Has the church ever played a documented role in helping homosexuals change their sexual preferences?**

# A

During the last decade self-help groups with a Christian base have developed. For example, Pattison and Pattison reported on a group meeting in a Pentecostal church that had successfully reoriented 11 males without any psychiatric or psychological intervention by professionals. They found that these individuals underwent not only a behavioral change, but also changed their intrapsychic views of themselves and their fantasy lives. Eight of these people had little observable neurotic conflict after reorientation. Six of the persons studied were married and did not report any problems with relationships or sexual adjustment.[55] Pattison and Pattison's paper includes an excellent discussion of the role that the church played in this transformation.

## Q

**Are there any Christian self-help groups for homosexuals?**

## A

Many self-help groups have developed either locally or nationally. One of the successful ones is Homosexuals Anonymous. HA is a Christian fellowship of men and women who have chosen to help each other live free from homosexuality. The purpose of HA is to support individuals seeking that freedom through weekly group meetings. Guidance is received through the shared experiences and growth of others. HA members gain strength by training their faith response through the 14 Steps of HA which lead, through integration with weekly experience, to a new perception of God, self and the world. Because HA is a self-help group, the members themselves, who have experienced significant growth, accept responsibility for different aspects of the chapter's organization and meetings.[56]

## Q

**How do I locate Christian ministries that serve homosexuals?**

## A

Exodus International is an umbrella organization for a number of ministries that are "dedicated to leading homosexuals out of bondage and into liberating union with Jesus Christ. God can restore the homosexual to wholeness! Exodus seeks to equip and unify agencies and individuals to effectively communicate that message to the homosexual." It maintains a referral list of qualified ministries. (For addresses and phone numbers of HA and Exodus International see the notes at the end of this chapter.)[57]

# Q

**Do any individual characteristics make successful sexual reorientation most likely?**

# A

No matter what type of therapy is used, factors besides motivation are involved. Prognosis is good in (1) young homosexuals, (2) those with previous heterosexual experience, (3) those who have recently begun homosexual activity and (4) those with aggressive personality patterns. The prognosis is poor in those who are passive and effeminate males.

# Q

**What can we conclude from all these studies of possible psychological and biological causes of homosexuality?**

# A

Homosexuality is a problem of sexual object choice. The experience of many investigators and therapists strongly implicates disturbed parental relationships with the child and significant others in the nurturing environment, as well as between significant others. I use the term *significant others* because grandparents, uncles, aunts, cousins and siblings can be primarily or secondarily involved. The significant "trauma" probably occurs during the first two to four years of life. This "trauma" is outside of the patient's conscious awareness, and cannot be remembered. There is no evidence that genetic or hormonal factors play any role in the development of homosexuality.

# Q

**What hope can homosexuals find in these scientific studies?**

# A

Treatment using dynamic individual psychotherapy, group therapy, aversion therapy and psychotherapy with an integration of Christian interventions will produce object choice reorientation in a high percentage of homosexuals. Successful therapy depends on high levels of motivation, previous successful heterosexual performance and aggressive, masculine behavior in males. Religious conversion may instantly reorient some persons. Christian self-help groups are remarkably effective in completely reorienting homosexuals who are adequately motivated.

Although homosexuality has its origin in disturbed family dynamics during early childhood, it can nevertheless be treated successfully. Homosexuals can change their orientation. God has condemned homosexual behavior and has made the power to change available to all who desire it .

# Bibliography

## Chapter 1

Acquired Immune Deficiency Syndrome and Chemical Dependency, U.S. Department of Health and Human Services, Public Health Service, Alcohol Drug Abuse and Mental Health Administration, DHHS Publication No. (ADM) 87-1513, 1987.

"AIDS: The Growing Impact," *A Weekly Journal of Medicine, Health, Science and Society*, vol., 3, No. 22, June 2, 1987, p. 2.

"AIDS Turns a Page," *USA Today*, vol. 15, No. 165, p. 2.

Antonio, Gene, *The AIDS Cover-Up? The Real and Alarming Facts About AIDS*, San Francisco: Ignatius Press, 1986.

Atherton, James K.W., "Surgeon General Koop: The Right, the Left, and the Center of the AIDS Storm," *Washington Post Health*, March 24, 1987, p. 6.

"AZT Does Even Better in ARC Than in AIDS," *Medical World News*, October 27, 1986, p. 8.

Barnes, Deborah M., "AIDS Stresses Health Care in San Francisco," *Science*, vol. 235, p. 964.

Barnes, Deborah M., "Promising Results Halt Trial of Anti-AIDS Drug," *News & Comment*, October 3, 1986.

Boodman, Sandra G. and Susan Okie, "Aggressive Prevention Efforts Proliferate," *Washington Post*, June 5, 1987, p. D-1.

Blattner, William A. "Etiology and Prevention of Acquired Immunodeficiency Syndrome: The Path of Interdisciplinary Research," *Journal of Chronic Diseases*, Great Britain, vol. 39, No. 12, 1986, pp. 1125-1144.

Boodman, Sandra G., "Born Dying: AIDS' 2nd Generation," *Washington Post*, March 23, 1987, p. 1.

Colburn, Don, "AIDS: The Growing Impact," *Washington Post Health*, June 2, 1987, p. 10.

Cole, Helene M., M.D., ed., and George D. Lunberg, M.D., ed., "AIDS From the Beginning", *The Journal of the American Medi-*

*cal Association*, Chicago, 1986.

Curran, James W., W. Meade Morgan, Ann M. Hardy, Harold W. Jafe, William W. Darrow, Walter R. Dowdle, "The Epidemiology of AIDS: Current Status and Future Prospects," *Science*, vol. 229, September 27, 1985, pp. 1352-1357.

Dan, Bruce B., M.D., "The Years of Living Dangerously," *Journal of the American Medical Association*, vol. 257, No. 10, March 13, 1987, p. 1357.

Dentzer, Susan, "Why AIDS Won't Bankrupt Us," *U.S. News and World Report*, January 18, 1988.

Farthing, C.F., S.E. Brown, R.C.D. Staughton, J.J. Cream, M. Muhlemann, *A Colour Atlas of AIDS, Acquired Immunodeficiency Syndrome, Ipswich, England: Wolfe Medical Publications, Limited, 1986.*

Finkbeiner, Ann, "AIDS: Just the Facts," *Johns Hopkins Magazine*, December, 1985.

Hale, Ellen, "An Update on AIDS," *The Montgomery County Journal*, vol. 14, No. 208, April 7, 1987, p. 2.

Koop, C. Everett, M.D., Sc.D., *Surgeon General's Report on Acquired Immune Deficiency Syndrome*, Washington, D.C.: U.S. Public Health Service, March, 1986.

Lifson, Alan R., M.D., M.P.H.; Kenneth G. Castro, M.D.; Eugene McCray, M.D., "National Surveillance of AIDS in Health Care Workers," *The Journal of the American Medical Association*, vo., 256, No. 23, December 19, 1986, pp. 3231-3234.

Okie, Susan, "AIDS Toll Masks Immensity of Threat," *Washington Post*, March 25, 1987, pp. A-1 and A-10.

Spechter, Michael, "AIDS Carriers May be Increasingly Infectious," *Washington Post Health*, March 24, 1987.

Squires, Sally, "Mental Factors Studied in Development of AIDS," *Washington Post Health*, March 24, 1987.

"Study Shows Lack of Information Heightens AIDS Fear," *American Medical News*, September 19, 1986.

# For Further Reading

Dixon, Patrick, Dr., *The Truth About AIDS*, Eastbourne, E. Sussex, England: Kingsway Publications, Limited, 1987.

Bradford, Rick, and Leonard LeSeourd, Betty Schonauer, The Rev. William P. Showalter, the Rev. Robert Whitaker, *Healing for the Homosexual*, Oklahoma City, Oklahoma: Presbyterian Charismatic Communion, 1983.

Cook, Colin, *Homosexuality: An Open Door?*, Boise, Idaho: Pacific Press Publishing Association, 1985.

*Facts About AIDS*, U.S. Department of Health and Human Services, 1987.

Hurst, Ed, *Homosexuality: Laying the Axe to the Roots*, Outpost, 1980.

Lovelace, Richard F., *Homosexuality: What Should Christians Do About It?*, Old Tappan, New Jersey: Fleming H. Revell Co., 1984.

Moberly, Elizabeth, *Homosexuality: A New Christian Ethic*, Cambridge, England: James Clarke and Co. Ltd., 1986.

Payne, Leanne, *The Broken Image: Restoring Personal Wholeness Through Healing Prayer*, Westchester, Illinois: Crossway Books, 1985.

Payne, Leanne, *The Healing of the Homosexual*, Westchester, Illinois: Crossway Books, 1985.

*Surgeon General's Report on Acquired Immune Deficiency Syndrome.* This 36-page brochure is available free by writing to: AIDS, P.O. Box 14252, Washington, D.C. 20044.

# Notes

## Chapter 1

**1.** Bruce B. Dan, "The Years of Living Dangerously," *Journal of the American Medical Association*, March 13, 1987, Vol. 257, No. 10, p. 1357.

**2.** *Ibid.*

## Chapter 2

**1.** This is not to say that a single person is less than fully human. It is to say that in the race as a whole males need females and females need males if the true potential of humanity is to be realized. All-male and all-female associations are bound to produce aberrations.

**2.** Kenneth Grayston, *Theological Word-Book of the Bible*, ed., A. Richardson (New York: McMillan, 1962), p. 12.

**3.** Derrick Bailey, *Homosexuality in the Western Christian Tradition* (London: Longmans, Green, 1955).

**4.** For additional reading on the subject of homosexuality from the point of view maintained in this chapter, see William Barclay, *The Ten Commandments for Today* (New York: Harper, 1974), pp. 94-173; Carlos Castaneda, *The Teachings of Don Juan* (New York: Ballantine, 1968); Henri Frankfort, *Before Philosophy* (Baltimore: Penguin, 1949); Yehezkel Kaufmann, *The Religion of Israel*, Tr. and abridged by Moshe Greenberg (Chicago: University of Chicago Press, 1960); G. Ernest Wright, *The Old Testament Against Its Environment* (London:SCM, 1960).

# Chapter 3

1. This passage is omitted from the best Greek manuscript tradition and is almost certainly not originally a part of John's Gospel; nevertheless, it is very probably a true story.

2. John V. Moore, "How My Mind Is Changing," in *Texas Methodist/United Methodist Reporter*, March 28, 1975.

3. *Ibid.*

4. Troy Perry, quoted by Harvey N. Chinn, *Texas Methodist/United Methodist Reporter*, March 14, 1975.

5. Moore, "How My Mind Is Changing."

6. William Robertson Nicoll, ed., *The Expositor's Greek Testament*, 5 vols. (Grand Rapids: Eerdmans, 1952), 2:831.

7. *Ibid.*, p. 839.

8. William Barclay, *The Ten Commandments for Today* (New York: Harper, 1973), p. 154.

9. John Boswell, in *News* (a United Methodist publication), September 9, 1975.

10. Matthew Poole, *Annotations on the Holy Bible* (1685, reprint ed., London: Banner of Truth, n.d.), p. 482.

11. John Albert Bengel, *Gnomon on the New Testament* (Edinburgh: T & T Clark, 1857), 3:22.

12. S.T. Bloomfield, *The Greek New Testament, With English Notes* (London: Longmans, 1839), 2:10.

13. Thomas Aquinas, *Summa Theologica*, 2.2.154.11-12.

14. *Ibid.*

15. Boswell, *News*.

16. Alex Davidson, *The Returns of Love* (London: Inter-Varsity, 1971), p. 44.

# Chapter 4

**1.** Altman, "The Movement and Its Enemies," *The Homosexualization of America* (Beacon, 1982), 112-13.

**2.** *Ibid.* at 113.

**3.** *Ibid.*

**4.** See *Are Gay Rights Right?*, Appendix C. p. 104.

**5.** See *Bowers v. Hardwick*, 106 S. Ct. 2841 at 2844 (1986).

**6.** See, e.g., Duluth Human Rights Ordinance, Chapter 29C, Duluth City Code (1959) (as amended).

**7.** Coleman, "Washington Gay Vote," *Washington Post* (April 21, 1979).

**8.** Socarides, "Homosexuality Concepts and Psychodynamics," 118. See also I. Bieber, "Homosexuality: A Psychoanalytic Study of the Male Homosexual," (New York: Basic Books 1962). Masters and Johnson, *Homosexuality in Perspective:* 399 (1979).

**9.** *Ibid.*

**10.** *Ibid.*

**11.** *Pierce v. Society of Sisters*, 268 U.S. 510 (1925).

**12.** *Loving v. Virginia*, 388 U.S. 1 (1967).

**13.** *Griswold v. Connecticut*, 381 U.S. 479 (1965).

**14.** *Roe v. Wade*, 410 U.S. 113 (1979).

**15.** See *Oklahoma City School Board v. National Gay Rights Task Force*, 727 F. 2d 1270 (10th Cir. 1984)--U.S.--(1985).

**16.** 106 S. Ct. 2841 (1986).

**17.** *Ibid.* at 2844.

**18.** *Ibid.* at 2844.

**19.** *Ibid.* at 2846.

**20.** *Ibid.* at 2846.

**21.** *Ibid.* at 2847. The Supreme Court appeared to follow the reasoning of an earlier decision in the District of Columbia Court of Appeals in which Judge Bork upheld the discharge of a U.S.

Navy Petty Officer who had repeatedly engaged in sodomy with one of his recruits. See *Dronenburg v. Zech*, 741 F.2d 1288 (D.C. Cir. 1984).

**22.** 741 F.2d at 1396.

**23.** See *Are Gay Rights Right?*, p. 44.

**24.** *A convicted child molestor—homosexual or hetero-sexual—could sue a day-care center that refuses to hire him because the center would be discriminating against him on the basis of his "sexual orientation"; such an ordinance would thus protect behavior declared criminal under state law.

*A hotel or motel owner could be sued under the human rights ordinance if he refused to rent a room to an unmarried couple that desired to commit adultery or fornication. This would be discrimination in the use of "public accomodations" (Alex. Code 12-4-8). This would also be discrimination on the basis of "sexual orientation," in this case their sexual preference for unmarried people or people who are married to someone else. Such ordinance would contradict state public policy by protecting behavior declared criminal under state law.

*An insurance company could be sued for refusing to extend health insurance benefits to cover as a "spouse" under the policy the sodomy partner of a homosexual or the other wives of a polygamous marriage. The insurance company would be discriminating on the basis of "sexual orientation" by refusing to extend coverage to "spouses" because of their sexual preference for same-sex partners or multiple partners of the opposite sex (12-4-8). Both sodomy and polygamy are prohibited under Virginia state law (crimes against nature, Va. Stat. 18.2-346) and such an ordinance could protect behavior declared criminal under state law.

*A bank that refuses to loan money to a moviemaker who enjoys making child pornography and selling it would be discriminating against the moviemaker on the basis of his "sexual orientation," his sexual preference for watching child sex (12-4-9). The making and selling of child pornography is a crime under most state laws. Such an ordinance could protect behavior declared criminal under state law.

*Law enforcement officials who arrest the customers of prostitutes, pornography stores or child sex rings could be sued under the ordinance as "obstruction of practices unlawful under this chapter" (12-14-11) if it is viewed that the police are discriminating against people who patronize certain "public accommodations" based on their specific "sexual orientation." This would be discrimination against those who have a sexual preference for prostitutes, obscene materials or child partners. Prostitution, sale of pornography and sex with children are all crimes under state statutes. Such an ordinance could protect bahavior decalred criminal under state law. See *Are Gay Rights Right?*, pp. 51-2.

**25.** See *Are Gay Rights Right?*, p. 54.

**26.** See *Are Gay Rights Right?*, p. 54.

**27.** See *Are Gay Rights Right?*, p. 21 and following pages and at Appendix F.

# Chapter 5

**1.** See, for example, Malcom Boyd's *Take Off The Masks* (Philadelphia, PA: New Society Publishers, 1984) and John E. Fortunato's *Embracing The Exile* (San Francisco, CA: Harper & Row Publishers, 1982).

**2.** Sylvia Pennington on the back cover of her book, *Good News for Modern Gays*, (Hawthorne, CA: Lambda Christian Fellowship, 1985) states, "once I believed that the Bible was anti-gay.... Through the years of prayer the Holy Spirit led me through every supposedly anti-gay scripture proving to me that God accepts gay people just as they are. Scripture never teaches that birds shouldn't fly or fish shouldn't swim. Today I travel the United States and Canada ministering God's love, affirmation and acceptance to gay people everywhere. I am still a born-again, spirit-filled, fundamentalist Christian and I could not and would not minister as I do if I believed God was anti-gay."

**3.** Barbara B. Gittings, "The Homophile Movement," in *The Same Sex,* ed. Ralph W. Weltge (Philadelphia: Pilgrim, 1969), p. 148.

**4.** *Ibid.*, p. 149.

**5.** See John J. McNeill, *The Church and the Homosexual* (Kansas City: Sheed Andres and McMeel, 1976), pp. 172ff., for a brief statement of the purposes and position of these two organizations.

**6.** Betty Berzon and Robert Leighton, editors, _Positively Gay_ (Millbrae, CA: Celestial Arts, 1979).

**7.** Eli Coleman, Eli, _Integrated Identity For Gay Men and Lesbians_ (New York, London: Harrington Park Press, Inc., 1988).

**8.** Paul Tournier, "What Is Mental Health?" _McCormick Quarterly_, (November 1965), pp. 39-46, 52.

**9.** _Ibid._, p. 39.

**10.** _Ibid._, p. 46.

**11.** Bennett J. Sims, "Sex and Homosexuality," _Christianity Today_, 24 February 1978, p. 26.

**12.** _Ibid._

**13.** Paul Tournier, _The Healing of Persons_ (New York: Harper, 1965), p. 183.

**14.** _Time_ (17 July 1978), p. 53.

**15.** _Psychology Today_ (August 1978), p. 53.

**16.** Alan Bell, "Homosexuality, an Overview," in _Male and Female_, ed. Ruth Tiffany Barnhouse and Urban T. Holmes, III (New York: Seabury, 1976), p. 139.

**17.** Walter H. Smartt, "Research Notes," _Family Life_ (April 1972), p. 10.

**18.** _Eternity_ (February 1978), p. 12.

**19.** William Muehl, "Some Words of Caution," in _Male and Female_, ed. Ruth Tiffany Barnhouse and Urban T. Holmes, III (New York: Seabury, 1976), p. 169.

**20.** _Ibid._, pp. 171-72.

**21.** _Ibid._, p. 172.

**22.** _Ibid._, pp. 172-73.

**23.** Alex Davidson, _The Returns of Love_ (London: Inter-Varsity, 1971), p. 91.

**24.** _Ibid._

**25.** Paul Chance, "Facts that Liberated the Gay Community," _Psychology Today_, December 1975, p. 55.

**26.** David F. Busby, "Sexual Deviations—A Psychiatric Overview," in *Proceedings of the Fourteenth Annual Convention of the Christian Association for Psychological Studies* (April 1967), pp. 55-60.

**27.** Bell, "Overview," pp. 141-42.

**28.** Ruth Tiffany Barnhouse, "What Is a Christian View of Homosexuality?", "The Pastoral Forum," Fall, 1987, Vol. 6, No. 3, p. 10.

**29.** Davidson, *Returns.*

**30.** John Patton, "The View Point of the Pastor," in *Pastoral Psychology* (Spring 1976), p. 242.

**31.** Don S. Browning, *The Moral Context of Pastoral Care* (Philadelphia: Westminster, 1976). See also Perry London, *The Modes and Morals of Psychotherapy* (New York: Holt, Rinehart and Winston, 1964) and Paul W. Pruyser, *The Minister as Diagnostician* (Philadelphia: Westminster, 1976).

**32.** Norman Pittenger, "A Theological Approach to Understanding Homosexuality," in *Male and Female*, ed. Ruth Tiffany Barnhouse and Urban T. Holmes, III (New York: Seabury, 1976), p. 166.

**33.** *The Book of Discipline of The United Methodist Church*, (Nashville: United Methodist Publishing House, 1984), p. 113.

**34.** *Ibid.*, p. 114.

**35.** *Ibid.*, p. 90.

**36.** McNeill, *Church and Homosexual*, p. 160.

**37.** Henri J.M. Nouwen, "The Self-availability of the Homosexual," in *Is Gay Good?* ed. W. Dwight Oberholtzer (Philadelphia: Westminster, 1971), pp. 204-12.

**38.** *Ibid.*, p. 211.

**39.** Robert Kronemeyer, *Overcoming Homosexuality* (New York: Macmillan Publishing Co., Inc., 1980).

**40.** See Jerry R. Kirk, *The Homosexual Crisis in the Mainline Church* (Nashville: Nelson, 1978), pp. 154-57 for additional suggestions along this line.

**41.** John F. Harvey, "Pastoral Responses to Gay World Questions," in *Is Gay Good?* ed. Oberholtzer, p. 136.

**42.** *Ibid.*, p. 135.

**43.** *Ibid.*, p. 137.

**44.** *Ibid.*

**45.** Howard Brown, *Familiar Faces, Hidden Lives,* quoted in *The Pastoral Counseling Review* (November 1976), p. 22.

**46.** John R. Powell, "Understanding Male Homosexuality: Developmental Recapitulation in a Christian Perspective," *Journal of Psychology and Theology* (Summer 1974), p. 168.

**47.** Sims, "Sex and Homosexuality," p. 28.

**48.** McNeill, *Church and Homosexual*, p. 155.

**49.** H. Kimball Jones, *Toward a Christian Understanding of Homosexuality* (New York: Assoc. Press, 1966), p. 81.

**50.** Busby, "Sexual Deviations," p. 60.

*51.* J. Harold Greenlee, "Strawberry Blondes, Southpaws, and Civil Rights," *Good News* (November-December 1977), p. 42.

**52.** Clare Ausberry, "Fear and Loathing: AIDS, Stirring Panic and Prejudice, Tests the Nation's Character," *Wall Street Journal*, November 13, 1987, p. 4.

**53.** Jones, *Christian Understanding*, p. 102.

**54.** Seward, Hiltner, "Homosexuality: Psychological and Theological Perspectives," *Bulletin of the Christian Association of Psychological Studies*, vol. 3, no.4 (1977), p. 2.

**55.** Mary S. Calderone, "Education for Heterosexuality," *The Journal of Pastoral Counseling* (Winter 1969-70), p. 9.

**56.** *Ibid.*, p. 8.

**57.** Powell, "Understanding," p. 166

# Chapter 6

**1.** W.J. Gadpaille, "Research into the Physiology of Maleness and Femaleness," *Archives of General Psychiatry*, 26 (1972):193-206.

**2.** R.V. Krafft-Ebing, *Psychopathia Sexualis* (Brooklyn: Physicians and Surgeons Book Co., 1933), pp. 335-52; Havelock Ellis, *Studies in the Psychology of Sex* (New York: Random House, 1936), Vol 2, 2nd part, p. 74.

3. Gadpaille, "Maleness and Femaleness," p. 193.

4. R. Green, L.E. Newman and R. Stoller, "Treatment of Boyhood Transsexualism," *Archives of General Psychiatry*, 26 (1972):213-17.

5. G.W. Harris, "Sex Hormones, Brain Development and Brain Function," *Endocrinology*, 75 (1964):627-48.

6. C.H. Phoenix et al., "Organizing Action of Prenatally Administered Testosterone Proprionate on the Tissues Mediating Maturing Behavior in the Female Guinea Pig," *Endocrinololgy*, 65 (1959):369-82.

7. Corinne Hutt, "Neuroendocrinological, Behavioral and Intellectual Aspects of Sexual Differentiation in Human Development," in *Gender Differences: Their Ontogeny and Significance*, eds. C. Ounstead and D.C. Taylor (Baltimore: Williams, 1973), pp. 73-121.

8. J. Money, J.G. Hampson and J.L. Hampson, "An Examination of Some Basic Sexual Concepts: The Evidence of Human Hermaphroditism," *Johns Hopkins Medical Journal*, 97 (1955):301-19.

9. D.B. Lynn, "A Note on Sex Differences in the Development of Masculine and Feminine Identification," *Psychological Review*, 66 (1959):126-35.

10. Gadpaille, "Maleness and Femaleness," p. 195.

11. See Hutt, "Sexual Differentiation," for a detailed bibliography.

12. *Ibid.*, p. 112.

13. F.J. Kallman, "Comparative Twin Study on the Genetic Aspects of Homosexuality," *Journal of Nervous and Mental Disease*, 115 (1952), pp. 283-98; E.D. Eckert, T.J. Bouchard, J. Bolen and L.L. Heston, "Homosexuality in Monozygotic Twins Reared Apart," *British Journal of Psychiatry*, 148 (1986):421-25.

14. Gadpaille, "Maleness and Femaleness," pp. 197-200.

15. *Ibid.*, p. 198. See also Gadpaille's comprehensive bibliography.

16. V. Halbreich, S. Segal and I. Chowers, "Day to Day Variations in Serum Levels of Follicule-Stimulating Hormone and Luteinizing Hormone in Homosexual Males," *Biological Psychiatry*, 13 (1978):541-49.

17. P.G. Doerr et al., a "Plasma Testosterone, Estradiol and Semen Analysis in Male Homosexuals," *Archives of General Psychiatry*, 29 (1973):829-33; C.R. Kolodny et al., "Plasma, Gonadotropin and Prolactin in Male Homosexuals," *Lancet*, 2 (1972):1170-74; L. Gooren, "The Neuroendocrine Response of Luteinizing Hormone to Estrogen Administration in Heterosexual, Homosexual and Transexual Subjects," *Journal of Clinical Endocrinology*, 63 (1986):583-88.

18. J. Loraine et al., "Patterns of Hormone Excretion in Male and Female Homosexuals," *Nature*, 234 (1971):552-55; Kolodny et al., "Plasma Testosterone and Semen Analysis in Male Homosexuals," *New England Journal of Medicine*, 285 (1971):1170-74.

19. C.J. Migeon, M.A. Rivarola and M.G. Forrest, "Studies on Androgens in Transsexual Subjects: Effects of Estrogen Therapy," *Johns Hopkins Medical Journal*, 123 (1968):128-33.

20. L. Starka, I. Sipova and J. Hynie, "Plasma Testosterone in Male Transsexuals and Homosexuals," *Journal of Sexual Research*, 11 (1975):134-38; D. Barlow et al. "Plasma Testosterone Levels in Homosexual Men," *Archives of Sexual Behavior*, 3 (1974):571-75; R. Pillard, R. Rose and M. Sherwood, "Plasma Testosterone Levels in Homosexual Men," *Archives of Sexual Behavior*, 3 (1974):453-58; G. Tourney and L. Hatfield, "Androgen Metabolism in Schizophrenics, Homosexuals and Controls," *Biological Psychiatry*, 6 (1973):23-26; W.H. Masters and V.E. Johnson, *Homosexuality in Perspective*, (Boston: Little Brown,1979):409-11.

21. W.W.K. Zung and W.P. Wilson, "Response to Auditory Stimulation During Sleep," *Archives of General Psychiatry*, 4 (1961), pp. 548-52.

22. W.P. Wilson, W.W.K. Zung and J.C.M. Lee, "Arousal from Sleep of Male Homosexuals," *Biological Psychiatry*, 6 (1973):81-84.

23. W.H. Masters and V.E. Johnson, *Homosexuality in Perspective*, p. 142.

24. Gadpaille, "Maleness and Femaleness," p. 200.

**25.** G. Schmidt, S. Sigusch and S. Schaefer, "Responses to Reading Erotic Stories," *Archives of Sexual Behavior*, 2 (1973):181-99.

**26.** Richard Green, *The Sissy Boy Syndrome and the Development of Homosexuality*, (New Haven, CT: Yale University Press, 1987), p. 61.

**27.** J.F. Oliven, *Sexual Hygiene and Pathology*, (Philadelphia: Lippincott, 1955), p. 577.

**28.** S. Hadden, "Treatment of Male Homosexuals in Groups," *International Journal of Psychiatry*, 16 (1966):13-22; E. Bergler, *Homosexuality: Disease or Way of Life*, (New York: Hill and Wang Inc., 1957), pp. 188-89; C.W. Socarides, *The Overt Homosexual*, (New York: Grune and Stratton, 1968), pp. 105-207; L. Hatterer, *Changing Homosexuality in the Male*, (New York: McGraw-Hill, 1970), pp. 317-87; K. Freund, "Diagnosing Homo- or Heterosexuality and Erotic Age Preference by Means of Psycholophysiological Test," *Behavior Research and Therapy*, 5 (1967):209-28; G.A. Rekers, O.I. Lovas and B. Low, "The Behavioral Treatment of a Transsexual Boy," *Journal of Abnormal Child Psychology*, (1977):99-116.

**29.** C.W. Socarides, *Homosexuality*, (New York: Jason Aronson, 1978), pp. 1-47; I. Bieber, *Homosexuality: A Psychoanalytic Study*, (New York: Basic Books, 1962), pp. 1-207.

**30.** R.J. Stoller, *Sex and Gender*, (New York: Science House, 1968), Vol. 1; R.J. Stoller, *Sex and Gender*, (London: Hogarth Press, 1975), Vol 2; D.J. Futuyma and S.J. Risch, "Sexual Orientation, Sociobiology and Evolution," *J. Homosexuality*, 9 (1983-4), pp. 157-68; R.J. Stoller and G. Herdt, "Theories of Origins of Male Homosexuality," *Archives of General Psychiatry*, Vol. 42 (1985):399-404.

**31.** E. Moberly, *Psychogenesis* (London: Routledge and Kegan Paul, 1983), pp. 25-38.

**32.** R. Green, *The Sissy Boy Syndrome*, p. 16.

**33.** M.S. Weinberg and C.J. Williams, *Male Homosexuals: Their Problems and Adaptations* (New York: Penguin, 1975), p. 102.

**34.** M.F. Myers, "Common Psychiatric Problems in Homosexual Men and Women Consulting Family Physicians," *Canadian Medical Association Journal*, 34 (1980):72-80.

**35.** S. Israelstam and S. Lambert, "Homosexuality and Alcohol: Observations and Research After the Psychoanalytic Era." *International Journal of the Addictions*, 21 (1986):509-37.

**36.** J. Raboch and I. Sipova, "Intelligence in Homosexuals, Transsexuals and Hypogonadotropic Eunuchoids," *Journal of Sexual Research*, 10 (1974):156-61.

**37.** T.G. Grygier, "Psychometric Aspects of Homosexuality," *Journal of Mental Science*, 103 (1957):514-26.

**38.** R. Green, *The "Sissy Boy Syndrome,"* p. 248.

**39.** M. Siegelman, "Adjustment of Male Homosexuals and Heterosexuals," *Archives of Sexual Behavior*, 2 (1972), 9-25; "Psychological Adjustment of Homosexual and Heterosexual Men: A Gross National Replication," *Archives of Sexual Behavior*, 7 (1978):1-11.

**40.** E. Hooker, "The Adjustment of the Male Overt Homosexual," *The Problem of Homosexuality in Modern Society*, ed. H.M. Ruitbeek (New York: Dalton 1963), pp. 141-61; E. Hooker, "Male Homosexuals and Their Worlds," *Sexual Inversion: The Multiple Roots of Homosexuality*, ed. J. Marmor, (New York: Basic Books 1965), pp. 83-107.

**41.** J. Marmor, "Homosexual and Sexual Orientation Disturbances," *Comprehensive Textbook of Psychiatry*, eds. A.M. Freedman, I. Kaplan and J3.J. Sadock (Baltimore: Williams, 1975):1510-20.

**42.** D.A. Hirsch and R.W. Enloe, "The Effects of the Acquired Immune Deficiency Syndrome on the Gay Lifestyle and the Gay Individual." *Annals of the New York Academy of Sciences*, 437 (1984):273-82.

**43.** F. W. Furlong, "Determinism and Free Will: Review of the Literature," *American Journal of Psychiatry*, 138 (1981):435-39.

**44.** I. Bieber, *Homosexuality: A Psychoanalytic Study* (New York: Basic Books, 1962), pp. 301-2; C. W. Socarides, *The Overt Homosexual*, (New York: Grune and Stratton, 1968):105-207; Albert Ellis, "The Use of Psychotherapy with Homosexuals," *Mattachine Review*, 2 (1956):14-16; J. Marmor, "Notes on Psychodynamic Aspects of Homosexuality," *National Institute Mental Health Task Force on Homosexuality*, (Rockville, MD: National Institute of Mental Health, 1972).

**45.** J.C. Finney, "Homosexuality Treated With Combined

Therapy," *Journal of Social Therapy*, 6 (1960):27-34; E.E. Mintz, "Overt Male Homosexuality in Combined Group and Individual Treatment," *Journal of Consulting Psychology*, 30 (1966):193-98.

46. R.T. Barnhouse, "Homosexuality," *Anglican Theological Review*, Supplementary Series, 6 (1976):107-34.

47. E. Moberly, *Psychogenesis*:67-77.

48. S.B. Hadden, "Group Psychotherapy of Male Homosexuals," *Current Psychiatric Therapies*, 6 (1966):177-86.

49. J.D. Frank, "Treatment of Homosexuals," *National Institute of Mental Health Task Force on Homosexuality*, (Rockville, MD: National Institute of Mental Health, 1972) pp. 63-68; A.B. Smith and A. Bassin, "Group Therapy with Homosexuals," *Social Therapy*, 5 (1959):225-32.

50. M.P. Feldman and M.J. MacCullough, "The Application of Anticipatory Avoidance Learning to the Treatment of Homosexuality I.: Theory, Technique and Preliminary Results," *Behavior Research and Therapy*, 2 (1965):165-83; M.P. Feldman et al., "The Application of Anticipatory Avoidance Learning to the Treatment of Homosexuality III. The Sexual Orientation Method," *Behavior Research and Therapy*, 4 (1966):289-99.

51. J. Srnge and K. Freund, "Treatment of Male Homosexuality Through Conditioning," *International Journal of Sexology*, 7 (1953):92-93.

52. G.A. Rekers, *Shaping Your Child's Sexual Identity*, (Grand Rapids: Baker Book House, 1982).

53. W.H. Masters and V.E. Johnson, *Homosexuality in Perspective*, pp. 1-411.

54. W.P. Wilson and R. Abarno, "Christian and Homosexual: A Contradiction," *The Bulletin: Christian Association for Psychological Studies*, 4 (1978):21-24.

55. E.M. Pattison and M.L. Pattison, "'Ex-Gays': Religiously Mediated Change in Homosexuals," *American Journal of Psychiatry*, 137 (1980):1553-62.

56. Homosexuals Anonymous
c/o Quest Learning Center
P.O. Box 7881
Reading, PA 19603
(215)376-1146

**57.** Exodus International-North America
P.O. Box 2121
San Rafael, CA 94912
(415)454-1017